THREE
DIFFERENT
WORLDS

THREE DIFFERENT WORLDS

WOMEN, MEN, AND CHILDREN IN AN INDUSTRIALIZING COMMUNITY

Frances Abrahamer Rothstein

Contributions in Family Studies, Number 7

GREENWOOD PRESS
Westport, Connecticut • London, England

#8431619

Library of Congress Cataloging in Publication Data

Rothstein, Frances.
    Three different worlds.

    (Contributions in family studies, ISSN 0147-1023 ;
no. 7)
    Bibliography: p.
    Includes index.
    1. Mazatecochco (Mexico)—Economic conditions.
2. Mazatecochco (Mexico)—Social conditions.   I. Title.
II. Series.
HC138.M33R67   306′.3′097247   82-6216
ISBN 0-313-22594-X (lib. bdg.)   AACR2

Library of Congress Catalog Card Number: 82-6216
ISBN: 0-313-22594-X
ISSN: 0147-1023

First published in 1982

Greenwood Press
A division of Congressional Information Service, Inc.
88 Post Road West
Westport, Connecticut 06881

Printed in the United States of America

10 9 8 7 6 5 4 3 2 1

To
Bob and Jonathan

Contents

Illustrations

Tables

Acknowledgments

I wish to acknowledge many people and institutions that helped me in this work. Gloria Rudolf Frazier, M. Barbara Leons, and Arthur Tuden have, over many years, encouraged me and offered valuable suggestions and criticisms. During a National Endowment for the Humanities Summer Seminar, "Themes in the Cross-Cultural Analysis of Women and Society," Eleanor Burke Leacock significantly influenced my thinking about capitalist industrialization by suggesting important reading.

I am grateful also to the Department of Anthropology at the University of Pittsburgh, Towson State University, and the Wenner-Gren Foundation for Anthropological Research for financial support during various phases of the research.

My family, David and Sylvia Abrahamer and Milton and Lillian Rothstein, provided encouragement and much practical help. Bob and Jonathan Rothstein not only enthusiastically participated in much of the research but also provided comfort and reassurance. I am grateful also to Jonathan for his photographic assistance.

I am indebted to Hugo G. Nutini for introducing me to Tlaxcala. I would like also to express my deep gratitude to the many people at the Instituto Nacional de Antropologia y Historia in Tlaxcala and Mexico City and the many government officials who provided valuable suggestions, information, and letters of introduction. In particular, Yolanda Ramos Galicia, the director of I.N.A.H. in Tlaxcala, and Desiderio Xochitiotzin frequently provided valuable assistance. Most of all, I thank the people of San Cosme for their assistance, generosity, and confidence.

Introduction

This book is about capitalist industrialization and its effects on the women, men, and children in San Cosme Mazatecochco, a rural community in Mexico. Much of what is discussed here under capitalist industrialization is often viewed in terms of the concepts of economic development or modernization. Although these concepts are frequently used synonymously, there are important differences among them. Industrialization refers primarily to machine technology and the factory system. Capitalist industrialization focuses on machine technology and the factory system under a historically specific set of relations of production. Modernization and economic development are broader and more inclusive terms. Because they are so broad, authors do not always agree on their meaning and some, like Rogers (1975), use them interchangeably. Economic development usually means increasing productivity. This may occur through the use of machine technology but productivity can also be increased without industrialization. For example, irrigation or new seeds can increase productivity without the introduction of machines. Even where industrial technology is involved, many studies of economic development never mention the technological component. Modernization usually refers to an attitude or value system that is associated with industrialization or development. What are considered "modern" values range from secularism and scientific attitudes to achievement orientation and educational aspirations. Like development, the concept of modernization does not focus on industrial technology or the factory system.

The main theoretical difficulty with the concepts of modernization and economic development is that because they are so broad, they often include disparate processes which should be distinguished (Tipps 1973:222). A recent study of modernization in Mexico notes, for example, that "modernization *may* expand the alternatives available" (DeWalt 1979:251 stress added). A second problem with the concepts of modernization and development is that they are ethnocentric. Since the European experience is always used as the model of modern and developed, a Western or European model is projected on the rest of the world. One study of Mexico, for example, which ultimately concluded that the whole concept of modernization may be more confusing than enlightening (Johnson 1972:263), defines it as "the process by which societies become Westernized economically and technologically" (Johnson 1972:8). It should be noted also that the Western model used is usually a middle class model. Oscar Lewis, for example, who is well known for describing the values of the poor in the United States and elsewhere as fatalistic (1968), concludes his study of Tepoztlan by suggesting that the Tepoztecans have adopted only the superficial aspects of modern life (1963:448). He bases this conclusion on the persistence of a psychology concerned with living with problems rather than solving them (1963:447). He fails to see that this can be a modern adaptation to poverty. The ethno-centrism of these concepts is also apparent in their implicit view of industrial capitalism as the final stage of human society. If, however, one sees a dynamic in today's world, whether it is the Marxist dialectic or any other potential for change, the concepts of industrialization and capitalist industrialization are more useful.

The difference between capitalist industrialization, which specifies particular relations of production, and the more general term industrialization raises other theoretical issues. We can discuss industrialization without falling into the same traps of generality and ethnocentrism that occur with modernization and development. For certain questions it may be necessary only to distinguish industrial and pre- or non-industrial. In San Cosme, however, and for most industrialization to date, the effects of industrialization cannot be understood without taking into consideration the fact that it is capitalist industrialization. For the people of San Cosme, it is not only that many are working with motor-driven machines in factories, but also that these machines are owned by a class of capitalists. Even though the owners may be thousands of miles away in the United States, Germany, or Japan, it is their ownership and the system of industrial capitalism, rather than the machines, that have influenced the San Cosmeros the most.

ANTHROPOLOGY AND CAPITALIST INDUSTRIALIZATION

Industrialization and, to a lesser extent, capitalist industrialization have been the subject of much study by historians, sociologists, and economists.[1] Although anthropologists have studied some of the problems associated with industrialization, such as migration and urbanization, and the broader processes of economic development and modernization, few anthropological studies have examined industrialization.[2]

The neglect of industrialization by anthropologists is in part a consequence of the fact that until recently the underdeveloped world, the site of most anthropological research, was producing primarily raw materials and extractive commodities. Industrialization occurred mainly through the use of inanimate sources of power in agriculture and transportation and communication; the production of manufactured goods was minimal.

However, anthropology's neglect of industrialization is only due in part to its traditional confinement to non-industrial societies. Even when we study industrial societies, such as the United States, or semi-industrial societies, such as Mexico, we focus on the "marginal" populations and rarely use the concepts of industrialization or industrial society. In Mexico, for example, the favored regions of anthropological studies are still Chiapas and Oaxaca (Chambers and Young 1979:49), the two least industrialized areas in the country. Our continued focus on the least industrialized areas of semi-industrial societies, such as Mexico, suggests that it is not the nature of the societies we study that keeps us from examining industrialization but the nature of the discipline. Four aspects of the anthropological approach combine to make it difficult for us to study industrialization: the unit of study in anthropology, inductionism, eclecticism, and idealism. These aspects lead us to ignore industrialization where it exists and to favor the areas of the world which are least industrialized.

The Community as an Isolated Unit

Regardless of whether anthropologists study a band of gatherers and hunters, a peasant community or an urban streetcorner, we have tended to treat the community as an isolated social unit. Even when we recognize the importance of the larger society or environment, the *focus* of anthropological attention is the part, the local group or community, rather than the whole, the nation or the world.

In the past, on the basis of a number of studies of similar kinds of communities, for example, gatherer-hunter bands or peasant communities, we have been able to generalize about foraging society or peasants because the parts, such as bands, and the relations among them are very similar. To generalize about industrial society, however, we cannot merely add together a number of studies of similar communities. As Cohen notes, "an industrial society is not the community writ large" (1968:52). By its very nature an industrial society is composed of different parts. Each part relates to another in a specialized rather than an additive way. Whether we see the parts as proletarians and capitalists, lower, middle, and upper classes, ethnic groups, occupational categories, or any combination of these, they cannot be added up to make an industrial society. Thus, industrialization or industrial society cannot be studied from the perspective of an isolated community.

Under the influence of Julian Steward's ecological approach and the work of some of his students such as Eric Wolf and Sidney Mintz, within the last twenty-five years the practice of treating communities as isolated units, even in non-industrial societies, has come under attack.[3] Increasingly anthropologists are using what Schwartz calls the ecology-society approach (1978). This strategy stresses the links between a community and the larger society (Schwartz 1978:246). However, at the same time that anthropologists are pointing to the need to study extracommunity relations, it has been said that we are not trained to do this. Usually, the difficulties are seen as problems of method. There is often an implication that field work with intensive participant observation, the main method of anthropology, is not suitable for larger settings and we need to develop alternative methodologies. But is it a problem of method or theory? We can and should continue using field work and participant observation in a single community as our method. It is an "immersion in otherness" (Belmonte 1979:xi) that as Valentine notes, "extend[s] freedom from ethnocentrism beyond a value acquired from lectures or reading to the substance of living experience" (1972:39). It is a problem not of method but of theory. The community can be the site of our research and the object of our research can be the explanation of processes in a given community. But we cannot understand those processes without a theoretical orientation that goes beyond the community and embraces national and international processes. The method may take us to one particular place but our theory of causality must embrace them all. Furthermore, it must embrace them in a systematic way.

The ecological approach recognizes the importance of external factors in understanding a particular community but it does not suggest what external factors are crucial or why.[4] As DeWalt comments in a recent study which is based on the ecological concept of adaptation, there is considerable room for improvement in analyses which examine the relations between a community and external forces (1979:20). That there is still considerable room for improvement in such analyses is related to the inductionism, eclecticism, and idealism that characterize anthropological theory, including the ecology-society approach, and guide anthropological research.

Inductionism, Eclecticism, and Idealism

Along with the community study approach, anthropology also has a tendency to use an inductive rather than a deductive approach. Our view of the whole has come from inductive projections based on the study of what Cohen calls slivers (1977:390).

The ecology-society approach rightly recognizes that we cannot ignore extracommunity relations but, by not suggesting what external relations are most significant and why, the general must be induced from the specific. The view of the whole, therefore, is still derived from a particular community. This is apparent in the fact that anthropologists have usually found their external reference points inductively. Oscar Lewis (1952), for example, followed Tepoztecans to Mexico City to study the socio-psychological aspects of urbanization. Similarly, Manning Nash notes that he came to the problem of industrialization as a problem which faced non-industrial people (1967:xi). While this approach had generated a great deal of descriptive material on various aspects of complex society, because of its inductive nature we still have not gotten very far in our understanding of the relations between the parts and the whole. As Harris argues, "the whole must be grasped *before* the parts can be analyzed" (1979:155, stress added).

Sometimes, as is often the case with inductive approaches, research is guided by an implicit theoretical framework. The implicit, and less frequently explicit, frameworks that anthropologists have used to locate communities in their larger environments have often come from sociology, economics, and psychology. Anthropologists have not borrowed haphazardly, but have most often selected explanatory approaches that are eclectic and/or idealist. An eclectic explanation is one that says sometimes one factor and sometimes another is causal. As Harris suggests, "Eclecticism consists of the refusal to state what generally determines what" (Harris 1979:289). An eclectic model produces eclectic results. It is not surprising, therefore, that in a recent review of Mesoamerican community studies, Chambers and Young point out that there is still a great deal of disagreement about the causes and directions of change (1979:64). An eclectic strategy is similar to an inductive approach in that there is no overall theoretical scheme. Thus, it too is incapable of providing a coherent view of the whole which is necessary if we are to deal with industrialization or other processes that concern the macrocosm or larger system.

An idealist approach takes human mental experiences as causal. This contrasts with materialist explanations which see the ideal (ideas, values, attitudes) as reflections, rather than causes, of the material world. Frequently, idealist causality is hidden under an eclectic strategy. Cynthia Nelson, for example, suggests that no single element is responsible for the lack of change in the Mexican community she studied (1971:126). The emphasis of her study, however, is on such cultural beliefs as the conservative force of the community ethos and values geared to short-term goals. There is no attempt to deal with the more general problem in Mexico of lack of opportunity for peasants. Nor is there any explanation of why conservative values exist other than socialization. The question of why the people of Erongaricuaro are socialized this way and not in another way is not even raised.

Since it focuses attention on thoughts, feelings, and emotions, an idealist approach tends to direct the anthropologist's attention to the psychological characteristics of the local community. Induction and eclecticism have directed anthropologists beyond the community but they do not provide theoretical guidelines for analyzing the connections. Idealism provides a theoretical framework but it insulates the community and fails to explain why people in some communities have conservative values while in others they do not.

Although the ecology-society approach begins and as used, for example, by Eric Wolf, is a materialist strategy, ultimately it is often another form of eclecticism or idealism. Many studies which use the ecology-society approach stop their analysis with policies made at the national level. Thus, they explicitly or implicitly suggest that, in the last instance, causality is located in the mental processes of national leaders. Rarely is any attempt made to relate these decisions to international and national constraints which determine the nature of the alternatives. The isolated unit is enlarged in such studies from the community to the nation but materialism at the local level becomes idealism at the national level.

In sum, anthropologists have ignored industrialization in general and capitalist industrialization in particular because most anthropologists have avoided, through inductionism, eclecticism and/or an individual-focused mentalist approach, any strategy that presents a consistent and coherent set of patterns for anything beyond the community. Although this tendency will no doubt continue, the growing realization that external conditions are crucial variables to be considered has led to a concern with frameworks that begin, rather than end, with the larger system.

Since anthropology throughout this century has methodologically and theoretically focused primarily on the part, we must turn to the theories and models of other social sciences which have been concerned with macrosystems.

THE BROAD VIEWS

While the understanding of social change was the main goal of all of the social sciences in the nineteenth century, during the first half of this century the study of change was rejected. After World War II, as formerly colonial countries gained independence, concern with change re-emerged (Kumar 1978:122). Until the end of the 1950s, sociologists particularly advanced a number of theories regarding the changes associated with industrialization. These approaches, which were derived largely from the dominant sociological theory of the time, structural-functionalism, began with two ideal-typical extremes, traditional and modern or industrial.[5] To each extreme were attributed a variety of interrelated characteristics. The starting point was industrial society's occupational specialization and the application of science or rational approaches to production. In this view, specialization and rationalization then necessitate such other characteristics as universalistic recruitment, achievement criteria, and functionally-specific roles. Traditional society was seen as the opposite of industrial society. Not only were traditional societies regarded as irrational and unspecialized, but they were also characterized as particularistic, ascriptive, and having functionally diffuse roles.

The pattern of change was less often described or analyzed than the stages themselves. Several patterns of change, however, are apparent in the formulations. One theme of the broad views was diffusion of modern ideas, knowledge, and techniques from the industrial to the traditional societies. Whereas industrialization was seen as a process that transcended national boundaries, if a society did not industrialize, it was attributed to the resistance of an autonomous traditional society. One discussion of industrialization in the underdeveloped world, for example, refers to "powerful indigenous cultures" that are "antipathetic" to industrialization (Hughes 1970:11). The western industrial world was seen as worldly and giving; the non-industrial traditional world was seen as unworldly (or otherworldly) and receiving. Usually, no particular barrier was singled out as the main obstacle to industrialization. Causality was circular (Kumar 1978:57) or eclectic. Myrdal, for example, speaks of "interlocking, circular independence within a process of cumulative causation" (1971:386). Similarly, Smelser suggests that variations in the pattern of change can be due to: values; integration; backwardness; population pressure; desire for national prosperity; type of industry; tempo of industrialization; dramatic events such as wars, revolutions, and rapid migrations; and many others. He concludes that such sources of variation make it impossible to establish hard and fast generalizations concerning the evolution of social structures during development (1971:355). Often, however, underneath an apparently eclectic approach, values and ideas were given primacy. As Harris suggests for structural-functionalism in general, the idealist bias is implicit in the preponderance of mental items among the functional prerequisites (1979:50). Smelser's list of sources of variation has such a preponderance of mental items.

Among the many difficulties with the approach was the problem that the models of traditional and industrial society did not correspond to reality. As Kumar suggests, they were often imposed on the real world with only the most casual investigation or reference to that world (1978:116). This led to an exaggeration of traditional resistance to change or a neglect of historical circumstances encouraging resistance and an idealization of industrial society.

1960s Modifications

The most significant change in the 1960s was that the already broad schemes of industrialization were further enlarged. Industrialization came to be "simply the economic component of a larger process of 'economic development' " (Nash 1967:ix) and development became part of the still broader process of modernization. Earlier theories had dealt with these broader processes but industrialization was usually a significant component of their models. The later development and modernization theories often ignore it completely.

Although theories of development and modernization encompass a great deal more than the earlier approaches which stressed industrialization, including modifications aimed at some of the problems, there are many common threads.

In his discussion of development, for example, Irving Horowitz stresses the need to focus on multinational characteristics (1972:x) in contrast to the earlier notion of autonomous traditional societies. His suggestion that developmentalists direct more pressure on their home countries and less on the underdeveloped nations (1972:xxvi) indicates that he is aware of the international context of development. The basic theoretical approach, however, remains unchanged. Although Horowitz suggests concern with process rather than static equilibrium, he continues to treat underdeveloped societies as integrated structures which resist change. He is aware of variations among non-industrial societies, but underdeveloped and developed are still regarded as polar opposites. Most of all, like his predecessors, his approach is eclectic. He notes, for example, that "Countries may remain underdeveloped for opposite reasons" (1972:49) and he makes no attempt to describe and explain underlying similarities. Similarly, he suggests that some variables are more important than others, but the important variable in one situation may not be the most important variable in another (1972:341). Finally, although he is more aware of external variables than were the theorists of the 1950s, he takes an eclectic position on the role of internal and external factors when he suggests that the relative influence of intrinsic and extrinsic factors cannot be determined a priori (1972:397).

As indicated earlier, anthropologists too have revised their earlier approaches to take into account external circumstances. At first glance, anthropologists appear to have gone even further than Horowitz. External factors are often given priority in anthropological community studies. However, there is rarely a consistent and coherent analysis of the larger whole. In large part, this is because the mainstream macroanalyses on which we draw, such as the approach used by Horowitz, are themselves eclectic and refuse to recognize consistent regularities in the historical development of developed and underdeveloped societies.

MARXIST APPROACHES

As the eclectic weakness in mainstream approaches became increasingly more apparent, some anthropologists concerned with the relations between the community and the larger society began borrowing not from mainstream theories of development but from a variety of Marxist approaches.[6] In these analyses, local-level change or stability are related to the national and international processes of capitalism and imperialism.[7] Despite continued debate among the adherents of various Marxist approaches, there are several important areas of agreement which serve also to distinguish them from mainstream eclectic and/or idealist approaches.

The Capitalist Context of Industrialization

Whereas mainstream theories begin with industrialization or development and ignore capitalism, Marxist approaches stress the fact that industrialization began, and in most cases is still found, in a capitalist context. Marxists further specify that in capitalist societies the important relationship for discussion and analysis is that which exists between those who own the means of production and those who, because they own no means of production, are compelled to work for wages.[8] For Marx, capitalism depends on the coming together of capitalists and workers. He writes:

> two very different kinds of commodity-possessors must come face to face and into contact; on the one hand, the owners of money, means of production, means of subsistence, who are eager to increase the sum of values they possess, by buying other people's labour-power; on the other hand, free labourers, the sellers of their own labour-power, and therefore the sellers of labour. (Marx 1967 [Volume I]:714)

Industrialization, including machine technology and the factory system, developed in this social form of capital. As Braverman points out, "the social form of capital, driven to incessant accumulation as the condition of its own existence, *completely transforms technology*" (1974:20, stress in the original).

Since capital is created and expanded through the surplus labor of workers, capital accumulation requires a constantly increasing supply of surplus-labor. This leads to a second distinguishing characteristic of Marxist approaches.

A Capitalist World-System

Mainstream theorists treat development in different countries as unrelated, independent, and autonomous. Marxists, however, see a single capitalist world-system in which industrialization and development in Europe was fed by resources and labor from what is now the underdeveloped world. In this system, development and underdevelopment are two sides of the same coin. As Frank suggests:

> The metropolis expropriates economic surplus from its satellites and appropriates it for its own development. The satellites remained underdeveloped for the lack of access to their own surplus and as consequence of the same polarization and exploitation contradictions which the metropolis introduces and maintains in the satellite's domestic economic structure. . . . One and the same historical process of the expansion and development of capitalism throughout the world has simultaneously generated—and continues to generate—both economic development and structural underdevelopment. (1969a:9)

Different parts of the world-system have contributed in different ways towards the accumulation of capital in the metropolis depending on the time and the place. Two patterns, however, are apparent.

Since the Industrial Revolution most of the underdeveloped countries have been under a system of mercantile capitalism in which capital is created by middlemen in the sphere of circulation by buying cheap and selling dear (Kay 1975:101). In this phase of capitalism, the products of labor are commodities, but labor itself is not bought and sold. Peasants, serfs, and slaves throughout the world provided such raw materials as cotton, rubber, tin, and food products for the metropoles. Merchant capital created, expanded, or reinforced pre-capitalist and noncapitalist class structures, such as haciendas, in what are today underdeveloped societies while providing capital for the maintenance and expansion of industrial capital in the developed capitalist societies.

This pattern of merchant capitalism persists either as a dominant or subordinate form in many parts of the world. More recently, however, as capitalists in the advanced capitalist countries search for cheap labor, industrial or productive capital has been replacing merchant capital in the underdeveloped world. In the last thirty years, mining and other primary production have been replaced with manufacturing as the major outlet for U.S. and other overseas private investment (Helleiner 1973:23). For example American and Japanese garment manufacturers subcontract with Southeast Asian firms for the production of clothes. Baseballs, luggage, and other items are sewn together for American companies in Mexico and elsewhere. Labor-intensive segments of electronics production are done in Mexico, Hong Kong and other underdeveloped countries. At the same time, expanding agribusiness, large-scale capitalist farms in which foreign ownership also plays a signficant role, has made it increasingly difficult for such pre-capitalist forms as the peasant family economy to continue.

With the establishment of industrial production and agribusiness, producers sell not their products, as in mercantile capitalism, but labor power. Peasants, who formerly sold only their products, now become proletarians who sell their labor. Relations of production in the underdeveloped world have thus come to mirror the proletarianization in the advanced capitalist countries. Development (in the sense of increased productivity and growth of GNP) has even finally occurred. But, as Foster-Carter suggests, the dependent and extroverted nature of the Third World's insertion in the capitalist world economy is a continuing and defining feature of these developing countries (1978:65). It is necessary, therefore, to consider the differences as well as the similarities between capitalist development in the periphery and the core.

A CASE STUDY OF THE EXPANSION OF
INDUSTRIAL CAPITALISM

This book describes the lives of the women, men, and children of San Cosme and how they have been affected by dependent capitalist industrialization. In order to understand the depeasantization and proletarianization that has been occurring there over the last forty years, the first chapter sets the community in its geographical, historical, and political-economic context. Chapters 2 and 3 describe the peasant family economy and its decline. The next three chapters describe the three new worlds that have emerged as family activities have become separated into a private world of domesticity for women (Chapter 4), a public world of factory work and politics for men (Chapter 5), and a semi-public world of school and childhood for children (Chapter 6). Although these new worlds are very distinct, they are bound together by a common goal. In their very diverse ways, the women, men, and children of San Cosme are preparing for and responding to their proletarianization and the increasing demand for educated labor which characterizes contemporary Mexican industrialization. Chapter 7 analyzes the efforts of San Cosmeros in relation to the opportunities for social mobility under dependent capitalism and discusses the broader implications of this parti- cular case.

Historical studies of European industrialization have indicated many of the same changes that San Cosme is today experiencing: the domesticity of the San Cosmero housewife corresponds in many ways to the Victorian "lady"; the jobs of the men are also very similar to the factory work of the nineteenth century; their increasing political participation is also analogous; and the efforts of families to prepare their children for a skilled labor force are also very similar to the efforts of families in industrial capitalist societies elsewhere. Analysis of the data from San Cosme suggests, however, as Foster-Carter points out, that while there is a homo- ficence to capitalism, dependent capitalist development produces a deformed progeny (1978:65) with even more poverty and un- employment and less mobility. The conclusion discusses this deformation in Mexico and its implications throughout the Third World.

NOTES

1. Most research on industrialization has studied capitalist industrialization. Rarely, however, is the capitalist context specified.

2. Among the few exceptions are M. Nash (1967), F. Miller (1973), Klass (1978), and Minge-Kalman (1978).

3. See Wolf (1955) and studies cited by Schwartz (1978).

4. Another example of induction and the ecology-society approach is the author's earlier analysis of San Cosme (1975).

5. Two useful critiques of development theories are Frank (1967) and Tipps (1973).

6. See Foster-Carter (1978) for a discussion of two of these approaches, dependency theory and mode of production approaches. A third approach, imperialism, is discussed in the articles in Owen and Sutcliffe, eds. (1972), Radice, ed. (1975), and Dietz (1979).

7. See Safa (1976), Fernandez-Kelly (1980), and J. Nash (1979).

8. See Oskar Lange (1968) for a fuller discussion of the significance of this aspect in Marxist theory.

HIDALGO

PUEBLA

MEXICO

MALINCHE

TLAXCALA

ZACATELCO

TO MEXICO CITY
91 KM.

PUEBLA

SAN COSME
PAPALOTLA

TO PUEBLA 23 KM.

PUEBLA

N

MEXICO

MEXICO CITY

TLAXCALA

TLAXCALA
PUEBLA

San Cosme and Vicinity

1

San Cosme:
An Industrializing Community

San Cosme Mazatecochco is a rural community in the Central Highlands of Mexico. In many ways San Cosme resembles numerous other highland peasant communities described in the anthropological literature. Subsistence cultivation on marginal land with traditional technology is still practiced and was the predominant economic form until recently. As late as 1960, more than half of San Cosme's population spoke Nahuatl, an Indian language.[1] Much of the material culture in San Cosme is also Indian. Older women and a few older men wear Indian clothes. (Women wear a long dark skirt, which is a piece of wool cloth wrapped around and secured by a sash, and a white collarless shirt. Men wear white cotton pants and a white collarless shirt). Many of the houses are made of adobe. Women still make *tortillas* by kneading the dough on a *metate* (grinding stone) and cooking them on a pre-Hispanic hearth. *Temascal* baths (stone steambaths) are still used and many people sleep on *petates* (straw sleeping mats). According to the 1970 national census, a third of the population ten and over was illiterate; half did not eat bread; and almost half (46 percent) did not use shoes. These Indian characteristics, however, do not reveal the real character of San Cosme.

I first went to San Cosme, in June 1971, because I was interested in factional politics.[2] I was told in the state capital that the president of San Cosme had been ousted the previous year and that it would be a good place to study politics. During my first visit there, a stay of one year, I concentrated on local-level politics. The

Main Street, 1971. The building on the right was an old elementary school that was converted in 1971 into a kindergarten. *Photograph by the author.*

Billboard Listing the Factories in the Industrial Corridor near San Cosme. *Photograph by Jonathan Rothstein.*

level of political activity was indeed high. It became apparent, however, that the political activity was only one manifestation of a more significant phenomenon; increasingly the peasants of San Cosme were becoming part of the industrial proletariat.

The people of San Cosme have sold their labor on an intermittent basis for as long as they can remember. It is only since the 1940s, however, that some have come to rely primarily on wage labor in factories rather than subsistence production. As a result of the national textile boom during the Second World War and the lack of dynamic in peasant agriculture, a small proportion of men became factory workers in Puebla or Mexico City in the 1940s. By 1950, 12 percent of the economically active population were in the industrial sector. That sector has continued to grow so that by 1970, 27 percent of the economically active population were industrial workers.

Although by 1980 only 22 percent of the households did not have one or more members engaged full time in a non-peasant occupation, in 1971 when I first went to San Cosme more than half of the population were still peasants. Thus the time when they relied almost exclusively on what they themselves produced on their own land, that is, the pre-industrial family economy, is still fresh in their memories. These memories, which whenever possible were checked with municipal records, censuses, formal interviews, and other historical sources, and the data collected in 1971 provide a useful point of departure for understanding the effects of industrial capitalism. Furthermore, since some San Cosmeros still rely primarily on subsistence production, some of the consequences of industrialization can be assessed by comparing the peasants of today to the proletarians.[3]

Some years ago Manning Nash (1967) studied a similar situation in Cantel, a rural community in Guatemala. He concluded that the differentiation between *campesinos* (peasants) and *obreros* (factory workers) was small and that the factory workers were not separated from the campesinos in life style, social behavior, or personality; but he also noted that the small changes might, over time, have a massive effect (1967:118). The differences between the campesinos and obreros in San Cosme were initially not great, but some of these differences have created significant changes.

Even today they share many similarities. Factory workers, like campesinos, practice subsistence agriculture. In the early 1970s, on the average, obreros earned only 100 *pesos*[4] more per week than the peasants. For factory workers, as for peasants, the important kinship units are the nuclear family, the extended family, and the kindred. Barrio membership is relatively insignificant for both groups. Proletarians and campesinos both are more likely to marry a spouse and have *compadres* (co-godparents) and friends from San Cosme than elsewhere. But some of the differences, particularly the extra income and the contacts and experience of the factory workers outside the community, have generated greater differences. The income differential has allowed at least some proletarians to participate in riskier and frequently more profitable economic opportunities, such as new agricultural methods or investment in a taxi or store. Their work experience has broadened their social networks and their extra income and connections have made obreros the dominant political figures in the community. Factory workers use their outside contacts to gain access to jobs, to education, and to state and national politicians.

In the 1940s San Cosme was a relatively homogeneous Indian peasant community. Except for a few families that supplemented small-scale agriculture with a mill or a small general store and a handful of factory workers, San Cosmeros relied on subsistence cultivation. The economic differences that existed did not differentiate the community into discrete groups. Except for five landowners, with fifteen *hectares* each, the differences in landownership were small. Even the larger landholdings did not confer much of an advantage. Agriculture in San Cosme is not very profitable today and was even less so in the past when there were no roads and fewer investment opportunities. The small wealth differences that did exist were not conspicuously displayed. Witchcraft accusations were leveled at those who had more animals and/or corn, and as in other Mexican Indian communities where leveling mechanisms operate to minimize wealth differences, wealthier families participated in the more expensive posts of the religious hierarchy. Although these mechanisms may not have eliminated economic differences, they seem to have been effective in concealing differences and lessening cultural distinctions based on relative wealth. Power differences within the community were also nonexistent because before 1943 San Cosme was a section of another municipality, Xicohtencatl. Except for a powerless representative to the headtown, Papalotla, of that municipality, San Cosme had no government or politics of its own and all San Cosmeros were uniformly excluded from power in the headtown. People in the surrounding communities regarded the whole population of San Cosme as "dirty Indian bandits." Despite the numerous similarities that still exist between peasants and proletarians, by the 1980s there was little about San Cosme that was not directly or indirectly affected by industrialization and proletarianization. Today it is a heterogeneous community with significant lines of differentiation between peasants and factory workers, women and men, and adults and children.

THE PHYSICAL SETTING

San Cosme is a nucleated *municipio* in the state of Tlaxcala approximately sixty miles southeast of Mexico City and fifteen miles from the city of Puebla.[5]

As a consequence of its location at an elevation of 7,400 feet on the slopes of Malinche, the climate is cool. The temperature varies from an average low of about 40° F in January to an average high of 75° F in May. Even in May, it is not unusual for temperatures to drop, particularly during the night, to the high forties or low fifties. The coolness of the climate makes possible the cultivation of only those crops that are resistant to cold. Corn, beans, maguey, and squash are the main crops. A further consequence of San Cosme's geographical location is that rainfall is confined to the rainy season between May and September. Without irrigation, which only a few people have, San Cosmeros can harvest only once a year. The poorness of the soil and extensive erosion further reduce San Cosme's productivity.

Geography places San Cosme less than a mile from a new paved highway to Puebla and Tlaxcala and three miles along a partly paved and partly dirt road to another highway, also to the cities of Puebla and Tlaxcala. Tlaxcala, the state capital, is primarily an administrative and political center and contact with that city is largely confined to governmental business or education. Puebla is Mexico's sixth largest city and is an important industrial and commercial center to which people from San Cosme go to work, study, shop, obtain medical service, and enjoy recreation. Puebla's accessibility is increased by direct bus service between the center of the city and San Cosme every twenty minutes between 6:00 A.M. and 8:30 P.M. Buses also run from Puebla to San Cosme at 10:30 P.M. Bus service to Tlaxcala runs every hour during the day. In addition, buses run between Puebla and Tlaxcala on the new highway every fifteen minutes. From Puebla and Tlaxcala there are frequent direct buses to Mexico City, about two hours away.

POPULATION

In 1970 the municipio had a population of 4235 persons occupying a surface area of 1150 hectares or 4.4 square miles. This means a population density of almost 1000 persons per square mile. San Cosme is thus representative of the very high density of the surrounding area (Cline 1963:87). While the population of San Cosme has been increasing steadily for at least forty years, more rapid growth occurred in the late 1960s and early 1970s (see Table 1).

Analysis of the birth and death rates in San Cosme indicate that the recent rapid increase in population growth is due to a decline in

Table 1
Population of San Cosme, 1930–1980

YEAR	PERSONS	PERCENTAGE GROWTH
1930	1,680	—
1940	2,068	23.1
1950	2,517	21.2
1960	3,129	24.3
1970	4,235	35.1
1980	6,124	44.6

Source: The population figures for 1930–70 are taken from the Censo General de Poblacion for the years indicated. The 1980 population is an estimation based on the author's census.

Table 2
Natural Increase of the Population of San Cosme, 1950–1979

YEAR	LIVE BIRTHS PER 1,000	DEATHS PER 1,000	CRUDE NATURAL INCREASE PER 1,000
1950–54	52.3	23.4	28.9
1955–59	48.6	21.6	25.1
1960–64	42.1	20.5	21.7
1965–69	45.6	13.1	31.7
1977	56.1	6.3	49.8
1978	40.2	8.3	31.9
1979	32.9	6.8	26.1

Source: Municipal records of San Cosme. The 1977–79 rates are based on the estimated 1980 population of 6,124.

the death rate which was not followed by a comparable decline in the birth rate (see Table 2). The lowering of the death rate corresponds with the greater availability of improved medical care within the last fifteen years. One and at times two physicians have been visiting San Cosme daily since 1963. In the mid 1960s a public health center was opened in the neighboring community of Papalotla. In 1980 a physician established a private practice in San Cosme and for the last few years a public health nurse from the state department of public health has been visiting the community and supervising the activities of several auxiliary nurses who live in San Cosme. With the increase in the number of men working in factories and the increase in the number of workers covered by *Seguro Social*, more people are also eligible for treatment at the Social Security centers in nearby Panzacola and Puebla.

Even with their relatively slow population growth and before the rapid increase in the late 1960s and early 1970s, for an agricultural community with limited land resources, little improvement in production techniques since Colonial times, and increasing competition from large capitalist farming and industry, the population growth posed a severe problem. Of the 1150 hectares in the community, 955 hectares or 2360 acres are cultivated lands. If an average family of five consumes 3000 pounds of corn a year (Nutini and Murphy 1970:86), and each acre in San Cosme yields 1000 pounds, an average household needs almost three acres of land. However, in 1970 the average holding was only 2.9 acres. Although this represents an average shortage of 100 pounds of corn per year, it should be noted that it was less than the 900-pound insufficiency that Nutini and Murphy (1970) found for the area in general. This difference between San Cosmeros and many of the surrounding communities was reflected in the belief held by San Cosmeros until recently, that while they were poor in money they were not so poor in land.

By the early 1980s, however, population growth, along with a decrease in the value of their production caused by continued deterioration of the land and competition in the market from the more productive large capitalist farms elsewhere in Mexico, had led more than half (59 percent) of the economically active population to turn to factory work as their principal occupation. For the first time, the obreros outnumbered the campesinos by more than two to one.

POLITICAL-ECONOMIC CONTEXT

In 1940 San Cosme was part of the neighboring municipio of Xicohtencatl. No buses came to San Cosme. Men borrowed shoes from the people in Papalotla, the headtown of Xicohtencatl and the community adjacent to San Cosme, so that they could dance during carnival. Although the Mexican Revolution of 1910–1917 had led to the distribution or sale of the four haciendas on which San Cosmeros had worked, they did not receive any of the ejidos (land granted under the Agrarian Reform) which were granted to Papalotlans. Most San Cosmeros supplemented their small holding by working as peons on the lands of Papalotlans who worked in nearby textile factories but refused to allow San Cosmeros jobs in those factories. When San Cosmeros did get jobs as textile factory workers during World War II, it was in factories in Puebla and Mexico City. Even today few San Cosmeros work in the factories in the state of Tlaxcala.

With the help of the contacts made through factory work San Cosme was made a free municipio. Buses began to run beyond the center of Papalotla to San Cosme. By 1970 San Cosme had electricity, potable water, and a six-year elementary school. During the 1970s a kindergarten, a second elementary school, and a telesecondary school were built.[6] In the late 1970s phone service, which rarely works, and mail service were established. Almost every house has a radio and 50 percent of the households have a television. Many houses are now made of cement and many more people sleep on beds. Health services have improved and the mortality rate has declined significantly.

These changes are due to the concerted efforts of the San Cosmeros. They have built schools, raised money, and made numerous trips to state and federal offices to obtain community services and improvements. But the changes cannot be understood by looking at San Cosme alone. What they have been able to get and what they still lack is tied to the development of industrial capitalism in Mexico and the accumulation of capital at both the national and international levels.

Throughout the book specific changes in San Cosme will be related to the dominant mode of production, industrial capitalism. At this point, however, it is necessary to discuss briefly some of the significant trends in recent Mexican economic history which determine the context in which San Cosmeros live.

First, it should be stressed that the entrance of San Cosmeros into factory work in the early 1940s coincided with the beginning of what is often called the Mexican "miracle"—its rapid economic development. Between 1940 and 1959 there was a 3.6-fold increase in industrialization (Frank 1969b:299). Since 1960 the annual growth of the industrial sector has been more than 8 percent (Gollás and García Rocha 1976:424). It was this industrial growth that made many of the changes in San Cosme possible by allowing San Cosmeros to be absorbed into the industrial sector.

At the same time, however, although industrialization has been significant and has enabled a number of gains, capitalism by its nature assumes inequalities. Mexico is further characterized by dependent development. This dependence is apparent in the nature and the recipients of Mexico's exports, the extent of foreign investment in Mexico, and the extent of foreign debt. Dependent or extroverted development limits development and the extent to which all or most, as opposed to a few, can benefit.

Despite rapid economic growth, Mexico, like many other Third World nations, still primarily exports raw materials and extractive commodities. There has been an increase in manufactured exports, but there is still a substantial and widening trade deficit (Hofstader 1974:24). The sector of the economy that has been experiencing the most development—manufacturing—is also the sector in which U.S. investment has increased the most (Barkin 1975; Economic Commission for Latin America 1978:534). Between the years 1955 and 1965 foreign investors received almost $1700 million (U.S.) from new direct investment, of which they reinvested less than 20 percent (Cockcroft 1974:227). The trade deficit and loss of profit through foreign control is balanced by heavy foreign borrowing, an increase in which has led to amortization and interest payments on foreign loans equal to almost 50 percent of export earnings (Cockcroft 1974:303). The trade deficit, foreign investment and foreign borrowing mean that a large portion of Mexico's surplus is transferred to foreign shores. The transfer of a large part of the domestically produced surplus (to repay foreign debts and as profit to foreign investors) has enormous consequences for the class structure and the distribution of the benefits derived from Mexico's economic development of the last forty years.

The process of development often eventually permits the incorporation of newly generated underclasses such as the hardcore unemployed (Johnson 1972:295). But in Mexico, where development is constrained by dependent capitalism, the extent to which industry can absorb much of the population is severely limited. Capital-intensive and labor-displacing technology from the advanced capitalist countries, often via the transnationals, has meant that the rate of labor productivity has risen faster than the rate at which labor can be absorbed. At first glance, it appears as if the transnationals are creating a great deal of employment. In fact, however, since they are increasingly buying existing Mexican companies, they are generating less than half of what they appear to be generating (Juarez 1979:124). By employing primarily young women, who were not previously considered part of the work force (and thus increasing the size of the labor force), transnationals have also increased unemployment (Fernandez-Kelly n.d.:9). It should be noted also that although it is the more labor-intensive industries which derive the greatest advantage from production transferred from the advanced capitalist countries to the Third World (Fernandez-Kelly n.d.:20), transnational companies in Mexico are more capital-intensive than national companies (Baird and Mc-Caughan 1977:23). As a consequence of this pattern of development, there is still a great deal of poverty, unemployment, and underemployment.

Forty percent of the Mexican labor force is still in agriculture, although agriculture only accounts for 16 percent of production (Cockcroft 1974:282). Unemployment and underemployment have been growing. For 1977, one official study gave a figure of 57.3 percent (Juarez 1979:142). Among those fortunate enough to receive salaries, more than 40 percent receive less than the minimum wage (Vellinga 1979:39) and real wages have declined (Baird and McCaughan 1977:21). Contrary to what is often thought, the situation for professionals is also bleak. According to the Director of Orientation at UNAM (the national university), a large number of those studying will not find professional employment (Niblo 1975:114).

Income inequalities in developing countries such as Mexico are sometimes mitigated by government tax and expenditure policies. In Mexico, however, neither tax nor expenditure policies have been geared to a redistribution of the solid wealth generated by the country's rapid growth (Hansen 1971:83–84). New industries, including transnationals, are often given tax concessions so less rather than more revenue is generated. For example, in 1965 the state of Tlaxcala, in addition to having low taxes, gave concessions to industry for twenty years (Nava 1978:38). The greatest proportion of public sector funds has been spent on infrastructure investments for agricultural and industrial expansion. While some of the population have benefited from the shifting occupational structure, the main benefits have gone to entrepreneurs and the upper-middle sectors because wage increases have been slower than price and profit increases (Hansen 1971:71–77). In agriculture most of the public money invested has been spent on the construction of irrigation works that benefit large landholdings (Hansen 1971:44).[7] The extent to which the standard of living of most of Mexico's population has been raised through public-sector investment in social welfare has also been extremely limited. In the late 1950s, expenditures for education averaged only 1.4 percent of the gross national product (Hansen 1971:85–86), and despite an increase in social security coverage in the 1960s, three-quarters of the Mexican labor force was still not covered in 1970 (Mesa-Lago 1976:238).

In sum, as Frank suggests:

Industrialization, rapid as it has been, education, capitalization of agriculture, public works, and other 'modernization' measures have not so far been sufficient really to absorb the population increase, let alone greatly to raise the economic level of the peasant base. (1969b:315).

Industrialization in Mexico has undoubtedly meant gains. There are opportunities, but social mobility is limited (Frank 1969b:314). Capitalism by its nature differentially distributes the gains of industrialization even in advanced capitalist countries. Under dependent industrialization the disparities are greater and the gains for the majority of the population are more limited.

In view of the enormous inequalities and poverty that still persist in Mexico, the gains of the San Cosmeros are even more startling. That the San Cosmeros have been fortunate is apparent not only in their rate of participation in the industrial sector—in 1970 27 percent compared to 17 percent for the nation as a whole—but also to the extent they have been able to get community services. As of 1970, of the eight municipios in San Cosme's district, three did not have electricity throughout the community and six did not have potable water (Asamblea Popular de Tlaxcala 1970:7). In the state of Tlaxcala almost a fifth (18 percent) of the municipios did not have a general secondary school and 73 percent of the secondary schools were private, but San Cosme had a federal secondary school (calculated from data in Holt and Padilla, 1975, and Dirección General de Planeacion Educativa, 1975).

Although San Cosme's proximity to Mexico City has been bene-
ficial, the fact the other communities in the same region have not
shared in the gains to the same extent suggests that proximity
cannot explain their success. Given the limited mobility in Mexico,
proximity is not enough. Furthermore, despite the gains they have
made, San Cosmeros have also been limited by the poverty and
unemployment which is so pervasive in the dependent capitalist
development of Mexico.

NOTES

1. Unless otherwise specified the statistical data is taken from the
national census for the year indicated or from one of two censuses taken by
the author in 1971 and 1980. In 1971 every fifth household was surveyed,
yielding a total of 150 of the 817 households in the community. In 1980 the
same households were restudied with the addition of fifty more households. The additional fifty were selected by interviewing a neighboring
household after every third in the original sample. In 1980 a complete
census regarding living conditions also was done in one of the four sections
of the community.

2. The first and major period of fieldwork on which this study is based
lasted one year, from June 1971 until June 1972. Subsequent fieldwork was
done for three months from June to September 1974 and for another three
months from July to October 1980.

3. Although such comparisons are useful, it should be stressed that no
one, including peasants, has been unaffected by the transformation of
Mexico from merchant to industrial capitalism. See Chapter 3 for a
discussion of the effects of this transformation on peasants.

4. In 1971–1972 and in 1974 the rate of exchange was 12.5 pesos to U.S.
$1.00. In 1980 it was 22.5 pesos to U.S. $1.00.

5. A nucleated settlement pattern is one in which the population is
concentrated in the center of the town and the fields are on the outskirts.
This contrasts with a dispersed settlement pattern in which houses and
fields are interspersed throughout the area. A municipio is the basic
territorial, political, and administrative unit of the state as established by
the National Constitution.

6. In a tele-secondary school some of the subjects are taught through
television.

7. For further discussion of the government's support of large-scale
capitalist agriculture see Chapter 3.

2

The Family Economy

Until the 1940s all San Cosmeros were peasants. Today, while most young men and a few young women become factory workers, in the community as a whole 28 percent of the economically active population are still peasants and 39 percent of the households are headed by peasants (see Table 3). That is, they produce primarily for their own subsistence on land they own or expect to inherit. Although the peasants of San Cosme are strongly affected by the larger capitalist economy, unlike the proletarians who buy most of what they consume with wages earned from selling their labor, the bulk of peasant consumption is what they themselves produce. Since the bulk of peasant subsistence is produced by the family and for the family, an important clue to understanding the peasant economy lies in the structure and organization of the peasant family. Before examining the nature of the peasant family and the family economy[1] in San Cosme, it is necessary to question some of the assumptions that have often been made in studies of the pre-industrial family.

Much of the literature on peasants contains numerous assertions regarding the importance of the family or household economy and the integration, fusion, and identification of the peasant family and the peasant farm.[2] Despite such assertions and despite the importance of understanding this type of family in order to assess the consequences of industrialization, our knowledge of the actual workings of the peasant family is still very inadequate. Until recently, historians focused primarily on public events and important

Table 3
Occupations of Household Heads in San Cosme

OCCUPATION	MALE HEAD		FEMALE HEAD		TOTAL	
	No.	%	No.	%	No.	%
Factory Worker	87	47.5	—	—	87	43.5
Peasant	71	38.8	7	41.2	78	39.0
Homemaker	—	—	7	41.2	7	3.5
Miscellaneous	25	13.7	3	17.6	28	14.0
Total	183	100.0	17	100.0	200	100.0

Source: Author's 1980 census.

people, rather than peasants. Even when peasants were considered, the family was usually regarded as part of the less important "private" sphere, and consequently it was ignored or treated superficially. Most of the sociological analyses of the pre-industrial family were concerned with peasant society, "not to know the past," as Abrams points out, "but to establish an *idea* of the past which could be used as a comparative base for the understanding of the present" (1972:28, stress added). For this reason actual sociological studies of the pre-industrial family were rare.[3]

Anthropologists have differed from historians and sociologists in that they have been concerned with *knowing* peasants. Anthropological studies of peasants are rich in data on particular people, events, and settings. Often, however, anthropologists inappropriately impose on peasant populations implicit or explicit assumptions and categories which are derived from family life in advanced capitalist societies. Among the most common and most misleading assumptions, three (derived from the model of the ideal nuclear family in Western middle class society) are particularly important. They have distorted our understanding of the peasant family and since they distort the baseline, they are misleading as to the effects of industrialization.

THREE ERRONEOUS ASSUMPTIONS

The first assumption confuses the household and the family by assuming they are the same. In middle class Western society the most significant family unit, ideologically if not in reality, is the nuclear family. Because this middle class nuclear family is characterized by common residence, there has been a tendency to focus on the residential group in other societies as well. This stress on residence has led to a neglect of some alternative units and an underestimation of the diversity that underlies superficially similar units (Yanagasakio 1979). Anthropological studies of kinship often seem to go beyond residence and differentiate the household and family. But, as Yanagasakio has pointed out, there is no clear conceptualization of the two, and ultimately the family and the household are viewed as revolving around the same central point (1979:166).

The problem, as Yanagasakio suggests, is that too often we begin with particular units, such as the household, rather than the activities of a particular society. She urges students of the family to first identify the important productive, ritual, political and exchange transactions in a society and only then proceed to ask what kinds of units engage in these activities (Yanagasakio 1979: 187). She suggests that by so doing we lessen the likelihood of overlooking some of the significant units, particularly those that do not fit our conventional notions (Yanagasakio 1979:187).

Not only have anthropologists often confused the family and the household but our view of the latter is further restricted by our characterization of households. As Yanagasakio also notes, anthropologists usually use genealogical composition as the most salient feature of domestic groups (1979:184). Households with the same genealogical characteristics are classed together regardless of whether the social relations are similar or not. Again, this assumption of the saliency of genealogy underestimates the diversity of social relations underlying superficially similar units.

In large part the two preceding assumptions stem from a third assumption that the roles of mother, father, and children are basically the same everywhere. Until recently most studies assumed that a woman's role is always primarily or exclusively domestic and a man's role, whether he is a hunter, cultivator, or wage worker, is that of the primary "breadwinner." Similarly, children are usually assumed to be as non-productive elsewhere as they are in the United States. Consequently researchers have focused on the productive activities of men and the domestic activities of women. Rarely have they considered the productive activities of women and children or the domestic activities of men.

WHO DOES WHAT, WHEN, AND WITH WHOM?

As will become evident, the approach used here, following the suggestion made by Yanagasaskio, begins with the activities of peasants in San Cosme and then determines the nature of the significant groups. Then we can begin to examine the effects of capitalist industrialization on San Cosmeros.

Who Lives with Whom and Its Significance

A great deal of debate has recently emerged over whether the significant unit in pre-industrial society was the nuclear or the extended family. In a controversial book Laslett (1972) has argued that since the average household size did not vary much before and after the Industrial Revolution, even before industrialization the small nuclear family was an essential element of English society (Berkner 1975:721).

At first glance, the data from San Cosme seem to support Laslett's position. Most peasants live in nuclear family residential units. Furthermore, peasants are less likely than proletarians to live in extended family households (see Table 4). Even if one considers residential histories, as some of Laslett's critics have suggested, the statistical data support Laslett. The residential histories of sixty-five peasant couples living in nuclear family units in 1971 indicated that more than half (55 percent) had not lived in such units after marriage. The quantitative data fail, however, to reveal three significant characteristics or residence among peasants in San Cosme: 1) the expectation of residence in an extended household unit; 2) the insignificance of residence in family cooperation; and 3) the diversity of relations in superficially similar nuclear family household units.

Table 4
Residence Patterns of Factory Workers and Peasants in San Cosme

OCCUPATION	NUCLEAR FAMILY UNIT		EXTENDED FAMILY UNIT		TOTAL	
	No.	%	No.	%	No.	%
Obreros	25	50.0	25	50.0	50	100.0
Campesinos	66	68.7	31	31.3	99	100.0

Source: Author's census, 1971.

With regard to the first of the above characteristics, despite its lesser significance statistically, the extended family residence pattern was not unexpected among San Cosmeros in 1971 when it was predominantly a peasant community. The rule, as in many other rural communities in Mexico, was that when a son got married, he and his wife would live temporarily with his parents until the next son got married. The youngest son, distinguished by the Nahuatl term *xocoyote*, inherited the house and remained in it after marriage with the responsibility of caring for his parents. If there were no sons, the youngest daughter inherited the house and remained with the parents. Although the rule of temporary patrilocality was not always practiced, in 1971 the rule that the youngest son (or daughter) stays with the parents was very much in effect. It accounted for most of the extended households in the community. Genealogical studies and residential histories of ten sibling groups also showed that in 90 percent of the cases a married child, usually the youngest son, stayed with the parents. In the households where the youngest son had not remained, there were extenuating circumstances. In one family the youngest son married the youngest of three daughters and they moved to her parents' house. In another, the couple had moved to another town. There was only one case in which no child had remained. In that household the couple had only two daughters and the couple was still living with the husband's father when the youngest daughter got married.

Given the short average life span in pre-industrial societies, many married children could not live with their parents after marriage, especially where marriage is relatively late as it was until recently for men in San Cosme. But the expectation was that if parents were alive they would not be left alone.

The high value placed on someone staying with the parents or parent is indicated by the fact that in 1971 only 9 percent of the households consisted only of a single person or a couple. In most of these cases, the person, usually a man, had never married or the couple had never had any children. Where the couple had had children, the children were living out of San Cosme. Even when children moved elsewhere, they frequently urged their parents to move also. In one case where the parents would have been left alone, they moved with their son to Mexico City. In another case, the youngest daughter wanted her mother to move to Mexico City but the mother did not want to. In another case where the three oldest children were already livng neolocally when the youngest son moved to Mexico City, a teenage grandson went to live with his grandparents.

People gossiped about couples in which the youngest son did not remain with his parents after marriage. One man built a house for himself and his wife adjacent to his mother's house. Even though his older married brother remained with the mother, people frequently mentioned that the couple had moved out because the wife was unpleasant and would not live with her mother-in-law.

A majority of people do not live in extended family households at any given point in time and most people live most of their lives in nuclear family units. Laslett's stress on the quantitative data, however, ignores the expectation of extended family residence and the various times during one's life when this might occur. For some people such residence did not occur until they were older and they were living with a married son or daughter and his/her spouse and children. For others it was when they got married and lived with their parents or their spouse's parents. For many it was when they were children and they were living with their grandparents. Given these three possibilities, all San Cosmeros expected extended family residence at some point in their lives and many actually lived in such extended family units.[4]

That industrialization has changed this pattern was apparent in 1980 when some proletarians said they never wanted to live with their married children or their parents. One middle-aged proletarian woman said that rather than live with and depend on her children, she would get a room and make *pepitas* (toasted pumpkin seeds) to sell in the streets. Another proletarian couple had already purchased plots of land for houses for their two sons even though neither son was married and the youngest was only fifteen.

The second characteristic of the peasant family and the strongest evidence against Laslett's argument that the nuclear family is the same before and after industrialization comes from an examination of the social relations within and without the residential unit. As Berkner (1975) suggests, the real changes in family structure should be sought in the way kinship ties function rather than in the size and composition of residential groups. Laslett assumes that the residential unit is also the cooperating unit. The data from San Cosme suggest that: 1) Living together in an extended family household does not necessarily mean cooperating in productive, consumptive, social, political, or religious activities; and 2) not living together is often accompanied by such cooperation.

The overall impression that one gets from extended family households in San Cosme is frequently of separateness rather than cohesion. For example, in one extended household, the parents make and sell bread. Their son, who is away most of the year teaching in Northern Mexico, occasionally helps make or sell the bread when he is home, but usually does not. The daughter-in-law never helps make or sell bread even though the older couple sometimes hire a neighbor to assist them. The daughter-in-law and her children do, however, work in the family store. The daughter-in-law does not help the older couple in the fields, but the older couple cultivate the land given to her by her father. In another extended household, the older couple also has a store. Neither their son, a campesino, nor the daughter-in-law nor their teenaged grandchildren ever assist in the store. The mother of another storeowner, a factory worker, does the buying for the store and the son, his wife, and their children do the dispatching. The mother, however, does not live with the son and his nuclear family. In another family, the mother raises sheep and goats and takes them to the mountain to pasture six days a week. She is accompanied by a hired boy. Her married son, who lives with her, takes the animals to the mountain on Sundays. Neither the daughter-in-law nor the grandchildren ever take the animals to pasture. Although these separate activities might be regarded as economic specializations which are interdependent and which ultimately all contribute to the household, many of the extended family households in San Cosme have what Nutini calls *gasto aparte*. Each component nuclear family has a separate budget (Nutini 1968:208) rather than *gasto junto* (joint budget). Their separate economic activities go therefore not to support the residential group as a whole but towards the support of the component units.

The increasing separateness of households with proletarianization was also apparent in the fact that, during the census in 1980, a number of respondents when asked who lived in the house did not include all of the people who lived in their compound. Only those with whom they resided *and* cooperated economically were listed.[5]

The same independence is apparent in other activities. If there is a *fiesta*, such as a birthday, wedding, or one of the members of the family has a *mayordomia* (a religious post), the other members of the household usually help in the preparations but family members who do not live in the same house are also expected to help. In one family when a child was being baptized, the mother's mother and the mother's sister, both of whom lived elsewhere, assisted in the preparations. At another occasion, however, when the mother's sister was making *mole* (the traditional dish for fiestas) for the barrios's Saint's Day, the mother did not help her sister. The sister lives with her mother, her brother, and his wife and children; they did not help either. The mother went to the mountain to pasture her animals and the sister-in-law went to the plaza to sell *tamales*.

In a few extended family households the extent of interdependence and cooperation is greater. These households represent the exceptions rather than the rule. In these households the greater control of resources (usually land or wage earnings) by one household member is used to influence or control other members.

Among campesinos in extended households the person or persons with the greater resources is likely to be the mother and/or father. Parents usually give a plot of land and one or more animals, if they have them, to their children when they marry, but frequently, depending on the size of their holdings and how many children they have given land to, they still retain the largest share for division when they die or when their other children marry. The income from larger holdings, as well as the possibility of inheriting more advantageously, can be used to control the younger generation. For example, when she married, one woman received a plot of land and a cow from her mother. Her married sister and brother received similar cattle and plots. The mother still owns a herd of about twenty animals and three hectares of land. At one point, when the mother believed that her daughter-in-law had induced an abortion, she threatened that she would cut the couple off from any future inheritance if the daughter-in-law tried to abort a child again.

In general, the members of an extended family household do not necessarily cooperate. Even in situations that appear to be similar, for example extended family households with *gasto junto* (a joint budget), the relations may be different. The relations between a son who is a peasant and his parents living in the same house are different than the relations between parents and a married son who is a factory worker. Peasants often stay in the parental household because they cannot afford to build their own house. The factory worker, on the other hand, usually has sufficient resources to move out. Where the son is a peasant, most of the household resources are controlled by the parents. They make the major household decisions. The obrero is usually not economically dependent on his parents' land or other resources and often his income is greater than theirs. Consequently, the factory worker, and occasionally his wife, make decisions for themselves and sometimes for the parents as well.

Often the members of a common household do not cooperate, while many who do not live in the same household do cooperate. San Cosmeros frequently exchange labor, both domestic and agricultural, with non-household members. There is also a great deal of sharing of food. Relatives and neighbors are given pots of mole whenever it is made. They in turn give smaller portions of what they have received to their neighbors and relatives. Particularly for peasant families the sharing of mole is an important, and often the only, source of meat. In a household where there is an avocado or fruit tree in the garden, its products are usually distributed to neighbors and relatives in other households.

Proletarian families in San Cosme still practice the sharing of mole and garden products, but it represents a relatively smaller contribution to their diet. Unlike peasants for whom it may be the only source of meat, for proletarians it supplements the meat, vegetables and fruit they regularly buy. Increasingly, they hire labor to work in their fields, rather than exchanging labor with relatives and neighbors. This is part of a more general pattern in which proletarian social relations, including family relations beyond the nuclear family, are becoming more single-stranded. The work, educational, and political activities of proletarians are bringing them into contact with a more diverse group of people with less overlapping of ties. They have economic ties to some and social ties to others.

Peasants work on their own land, on the land of others, and in a variety of odd jobs. In the first situation, the peasant comes into contact primarily with his or her own nuclear family. If any additional workers are needed, the peasant woman usually exchanges labor with a female relative or neighbor. This economic activity brings peasants into contact with those with whom they already have social relations. The activity intensifies already existing relationships. Working on the land of others or other forms of earning cash, such as selling *pulque* (an alcoholic beverage made from the maguey plant) or assisting a mason, take place within San Cosme and thus also involve those with whom peasants already have existing ties.

Proletarian families, because their economic relations are often separate from their kinship and social ties, have a wider network but their ties beyond the nuclear family are less intense. Factory work, which will be discussed in more detail in Chapter 5, brings the obrero into contact with other San Cosmeros but it also extends ties to workers from other areas. Although factory workers sometimes develop relations of *compadrazgo* (co-parenthood), co-residence, friendship, and marriage, often they are merely fellow workers with no additional social ties.

In sum, peasants have multi-stranded relations with relatives and neighbors in San Cosme. Although the nuclear family is a significant unit, it is embedded in a web of family and community ties. The embeddedness of the peasant nuclear family and the expectation of living at some point with family members other than one's own immediate family serve to differentiate peasant and proletarian family life. These characteristics also suggest that Laslett's focus on kinship only within the residential unit, or the confusion of household and family, ignores significant aspects of the preindustrial family.

Economic Roles in Family Production

In a family economy where the family is both the unit of production and the unit of consumption, the lines between women's work, men's work, and the work of the old and the young are blurred. Although there is a division of labor by age and sex, in the peasant family men's work, women's work, and children's work are all part of a single process or continuum. Food is produced at one end of this continuum and consumed at the other.

This is apparent in the roles of men, women, and children in the production and preparation of corn, the staple of the Mexican peasant economy. Young and old, male and female, all participate in the planting and harvesting of corn. The men and older boys usually perform the tasks that involve animals—plowing, loading and transporting—and women and children plant, cut the points (to hasten the drying process), and cut the corn and *sacate* (dried cornstalks used for fodder and fuel). Women sometimes do the men's tasks and men sometimes plant and perform other women's tasks. Neither sex is ridiculed for crossing the sexual division of labor. After the corn is harvested, it is taken off the cob. Women spend more time shucking corn than do the men but it is not uncommon for whoever is around, men and children over the age of six as well as women, to participate. From this point on, women and girls are responsible for the cooking and serving of the corn, mainly in the form of tortillas, but males may at times also cook. For example, teenage boys frequently get together and cook corn on the cob.

The same pattern of overlapping spheres for men, women, and children is evident in other agricultural activities. Most peasant families have a few animals. Women and girls care for and women slaughter chickens and turkeys. Men slaughter and men and boys feed pigs, cows, and horses and clean the pigpens. Older men, older women, and boys, and less frequently younger women and men, take sheep, goats, and cows to the mountain to pasture. Frequently, a young boy will go along with an older brother, parent or grandparent.

In addition to planting, plowing, and harvesting corn and raising animals, agricultural work includes going to the mountain for wood, and going to the fields to cut *elotes* (corn on the cob), squash, beans, or weeds.[6] Any two or three members of the family, usually the nuclear family but not necessarily, might go together to cut cane, wood, and so forth. Picking fruit is also usually done by two or three family members. Men and boys are more likely to climb the trees but young girls frequently do so and whoever climbs the tree passes the fruit down to those on the ground.

Except for planting and harvesting when larger work forces are necessary, an entire nuclear family or household unit rarely all work as a group. Usually, however, more than one family member is involved and unless only brothers or sisters work together, this means the participation of both sexes and/or two or more generations. For example, when the chickens of an older peasant couple needed to be injected, the people involved included three generations, ranging in age from six to seventy, members of three different households, and both sexes. Three children—a granddaughter and two greatnieces of the older couple—ran after the chickens and caught them. The older couple's daughter injected them while they held the chickens and tied identifying thread to those with which they were finished.

Although men assume the greatest responsibility in agricultural production, women and children also have significant roles in production. Spot observations made during August and September, when agricultural activity is relatively light, show that peasant men, especially fathers, do the most agricultural work; but there was no family in which only the father did agricultural tasks.[7] In three of the eight peasant families studied, at least half of the

Peasant Women Returning with Wood from the Mountain. *Photograph by the author.*

agricultural activities done involved other family members. The spot observations also indicate that in only one of the families was all the agricultural work done by the males. Similarly, there was only one family in which all of the agricultural work was done by the parents. In this family the children were a married son who was a factory worker, his wife who did most of the domestic work, and three grandchildren ranging in age from one to seven.

The bulk of peasant subsistence is derived from the small parcels of land (one and a half to five hectares) they own or expect to inherit. In families with less land the father and/or a son usually become factory workers. Most of the obreros used their first earnings to purchase land in San Cosme or neighboring communities so that they could supplement their wages and, if they lost their jobs, could go back to a peasant economy. Peasant families with more than five hectares either had to eventually subdivide or they sold some of their land to the obreros just mentioned and converted their capital into a store, truck, or other investment. Thus, the peasants of San Cosme usually have sufficient land to provide most of their subsistence, but not much more. To supplement their income from the land and to cover such expenses as clothing, household items, food not produced, electricity, and educational expenses, peasants engage in a variety of other economic activities. These supplementary activities usually take the form of part-time sporadic jobs. Until recently this was equally true for peasant men and women. The main supplementary activities were working on someone else's land, selling wood and charcoal, and making and selling pulque. In addition, some peasant men are also musicians, storeowners, butchers, breadmakers, or masons. A few peasant men work on the alfalfa truck that comes to the community and some assist butchers, masons, and other local specialists. For peasant women supplementary economic activities include shelling corn for others, sewing for sale, selling flowers or eggs and, at fiestas, tamales or other prepared foods, working in the family store, and working on the lands of others. Because of the sporadic and varying nature of most peasants' supplementary activities, it is difficult to estimate the relative contributions of women and men to family income. Until recently, when the wage opportunities for peasant men but not for the peasant women increased, there was no prevailing view that one sex contributed more than the other.

Domestic Activities

Peasant women bear the main responsibility for domestic activities, but they do not bear that responsibility alone. Many of the domestic tasks are shared. Adult women, whether they live in the same household or not, frequently assist each other with childcare and food preparation. Children also perform a great deal of housework. Both boys and girls begin sweeping, shucking corn, and going to the store by the age of six. Girls and, if there are no girls or their sisters are unavailable, boys begin childcare at about age seven. Between the ages of eight and ten, girls usually start making tortillas and meals, going to the mill, and washing dishes and clothes. The importance of children, especially daughters, in domestic work is apparent in Table 5. Of the domestic activities reported in the spot observations, children were as frequently reported doing domestic activities as were mothers.

Another important characteristic of domestic work in the peasant economy is that because the locus of much of peasant production, such as animal raising, gardening, and making pulque and charcoal, is the house, productive activities can be performed simultaneously or alternately with domestic tasks. Furthermore, as Deere points out, since the producer controls the productive

Table 5
Family Participation in Domestic Activities in San Cosme

	NUMBER OF TIMES REPORTED DOING DOMESTIC TASKS
Mothers	30
Daughters	22
Sons	8
Fathers	4
Total	64

Source: Spot observations of eight peasant families.

process, there are no rigid work schedules and hierarchical structures with which to contend (1979:144). Childcare, for example, is almost always combined with other activities in the house, garden, or fields. Women are frequently seen in the fields with young children and men are often accompanied by sons of seven to twelve. Cousins and siblings often care for younger children while they work or play.

Authority Relations

In the peasant families in San Cosme neither husbands nor wives tell each other what to do. Inheritance is bilateral so men and women have approximately the same amount of land. Differences in authority are structured by age rather than sex. Parents often retain control of land and other resources and use these resources to control the younger generation. One woman described how in her first years of marriage her mother-in-law sent her to the fields every day while she stayed home drinking pulque with her friends. Daughters also often object to the great deal of domestic work that falls on them. As the authority of parents wanes or dies, activities are dictated not by one's spouse, but by the division of labor. Women do not need to be told to plant, nor do men need to be told to plow. In informal discussions peasants said decisions such as when and how much corn should be planted or sold are made jointly and are ruled by family consumption needs rather than by individuals. One peasant woman, for example, said that she and her husband usually decide to sell a sheep when they need the money for expenses such as uniforms for children in school.[8]

THE PEASANT FAMILY AND
THE LARGER SOCIETY

Peasants are part of the larger nation-state and are subject to the economic and political dictates that stem from outside the community. Peasants in San Cosme, however, have few direct relations beyond San Cosme and the surrounding communities. Their lands are within the community. Their supplementary economic activities are usually also confined to San Cosme or occasionally Papalotla, their nearest neighbor. Even though the alfalfa truck on which several San Cosmeros work comes from elsewhere and goes to other communities, the San Cosmeros work

Peasant Woman Doing the Laundry. *Photograph by the author.*

on it only while it is in San Cosme and Papalotla. The corn that they sell is sold to middlemen who come to the community or to local merchants. Most of their purchases are similarly made in San Cosme. Although all San Cosmeros tend to marry other San Cosmeros, peasants are more likely than proletarians to do so. According to the Civil Registry, of twenty-six factory workers who married in 1971, three married women from elsewhere. None of the eleven peasant men who married in that year did so. Their compadres are also more likely to come from San Cosme. One forty-year-old campesino, for example, has six compadres, all of whom are from San Cosme. A forty-year-old obrero had eight compadres: six are from San Cosme, one is a fellow factory worker from another community in Tlaxcala, and one is a tailor from the city of Tlaxcala. Because peasants lack other kinds of contacts to regional and national politicians, if they have any affairs that have to be dealt with by politicians outside the community, they go through a local non-peasant intermediary or broker.

Within the community, a peasant nuclear family is related to other San Cosmeros through a multi-stranded set of economic and social ties. Political relations, to the minimal extent that peasants participate in them, are part of these other economic and social ties. Since 1967 San Cosme has been divided into two factions. The active participants in the factions are obreros, teachers, or merchants, because local politics require contacts beyond the community which peasants do not have (see Chapter 5). When peasants do get involved in local political conflicts it is because they have economic and social ties to one of the active participants. Factory workers also get involved in local-level politics because of a combination of economic and social ties. More often, however, they become participants on the basis of only an economic tie. Although economic interest is important in peasant political activity, because their economic relations are more likely to be just one strand of a multi-stranded relation, their political relations are more likely to be linked to family, kinship, and neighborhood ties.

The family and family relations also structure the participation of peasants in the community religious system. Discussions of religion in peasant communities in Mexico have stressed the importance of the cargo or fiesta system in which community members fill offices responsible for the performance of rituals, often involving a fiesta or celebration, for the saints. For peasants in San Cosme as in other rural Mesoamerican communities, the cargo system is the most important community-wide system. Most discussions of the cargo system focus on the men who fill the cargos, how they are selected, the prestige they get, and the responsibilities and obligations involved.[9] It is important to stress also that, as in economic life, the important unit for religious purposes is the peasant family rather than the individual. The nuclear family of the cargoholder, helped by neighbors and relatives, bear much of the financial costs of the post. An important part of most fiestas is the serving of mole to other cargoholders, their families, and other guests. The preparations for these fiestas involve the immediate family of the cargoholder (spouse and children) and their sisters, brothers, parents, in-laws, and their children.

CONCLUSION

A superficial examination of peasant society suggests that, as in capitalist industrial society, the nuclear family is the significant unit. A more intensive analysis, however, reveals that relations among and within family units in peasant society are significantly different.

Among peasants nuclear families, which are the most common and the most basic units in San Cosme, are very much embedded in a wider network of multiplex relations among kin and neighbors. Regardless of whether they live together or not, the members of different nuclear families cooperate extensively in economic, social, political, and religious activities. The extent to which nuclear families are not and do not regard themselves as isolated units is apparent in the expectation that at some point in the life cycle one will live with one's grandparents, adult children, and grandchildren as well as one's parents.

Within the nuclear family, men, women, and children all participate in both productive and domestic activities. Productive, reproductive (childbearing and child rearing), and consumptive activities are continuous and compatible. Not surprisingly, given their interdependence, relations between the sexes are relatively egalitarian.

Increasingly, however, the subsistence cultivation practiced by peasant families is becoming less viable and more San Cosmeros are being forced to sell their labor on a full-time basis. As wage work increases, production, reproduction, and consumption become separated both physically and socially. The roles of men, women, and children become more distinct and their three different worlds become arranged in a hierarchial order.

NOTES

1. Many authors use the term household economy, but family economy is more appropriate. I am grateful to Gloria Rudolf Frazier for making me aware of this.

2. See Sorokin, Zimmerman, and Galpin (1930), and Shanin (1971).

3. See Elder (1978) for a discussion of this point.

4. This could be reflected in quantitative data, if as Berkner (1975) suggests, different questions were asked. Unfortunately, the residential histories that I have begin with marriage and end before the couples died.

5. I use "household" to refer to this group or the larger residential unit.

6. Most of the corn is harvested when it is dry in October and then used to make flour for tortillas. In August, however, people pick corn to be roasted or boiled on the cob. They usually pick only the amount they will consume for the day plus some to distribute to relatives or neighbors.

7. A modified version of the "spot observations" suggested by Johnson (1978) was used in 1980. Eight peasant families and fifteen proletarian families were each visited on randomly selected days by an assistant eight times during August and September. They were asked what each family member had been doing at a specified and randomly selected time between 6 A.M. and 10 P.M. The visits were made on the same day or the following day if the time to be recorded was late afternoon or evening. Seven of the peasant families and fourteen of the proletarian families were nuclear families. One peasant family included a peasant couple, their married son and his wife, and three grandchildren. One proletarian family included a proletarian couple, their three children, and the husband's mother.

8. It is very difficult to get good data on authority relations within the family. I cannot recall ever having heard a peasant man or woman tell their spouse what to do and nobody mentioned such instances to me. I did, however, hear proletarian men telling their wives what to do and some proletarian women complained that their husbands told them what they should or should not do. One woman, for example, said that she had wanted to study practical nursing in Puebla, but her husband had said she could not.

9. See Cancian (1965).

CHAPTER

3

The Decline of the Family Economy

In 1940 San Cosme was a peasant community. By 1980 less then one of every four households continued to rely primarily on what they themselves produced. When they talked about the future, some San Cosmeros—the more fortunate—could even see San Cosme as a suburb of Puebla. Most San Cosmeros believed that in the near future almost all of the land would be used for housing or factories and there would be little left for cultivation. Although most San Cosmeros see the decline of the family economy as a consequence of population growth, population increase is only the surface phenomenon. What is happening in San Cosme is part of the larger process of the expansion of industrial capitalism and the depeasantization and proletarianization of Mexico. Before considering that process it is necessary to examine the notion, common in the popular press and the mainstream social science literature, as well as among San Cosmeros, that the problems of poor peasants are demographic.

DEMOGRAPHY OR POLITICAL ECONOMY

Undoubtedly the birth rate in San Cosme and in Mexico in general is high, but economic growth has also been substantial. Since 1935 the Mexican economy has actually exceeded the rate of population increase by at least 2.5 percent annually (Sanders 1974:7). Peasants, however, have not benefitted from this economic development.

Conventional wisdom often blames population growth and land ıragmentation for the problems faced by the peasantry. Cline, for example, writes: "The pressure of this mounting population has put almost intolerable strains on the small and previously casually exploited natural resources" (1963:85). Few studies, however, actually examine the assumption that it is population pressure that is largely responsible for the inadequacy of peasant holdings and depeasantization.

It is very difficult to obtain accurate demographic information for the Mexican population, especially for the rural areas. The criterion used to determine "rural"—residence in a locale of less than 2500 inhabitants—underestimates the size of the rural population. It is also generally believed that vital statistics are not accurate. Births and deaths are not always reported and, in my experience in San Cosme, they were sometimes reported years after the event and reported and recorded more than once.[1] Surprisingly, as Roberts notes, infant mortality data are not reported in rural and urban categories in the Mexican census (1973:675). Despite these difficulties, there are hints that "explosive growth" (the phrase used by Lomnitz in an otherwise excellent book [1977:41] among others) exists more in the minds of social scientists and in the modern urban sector than in the Mexican countryside.

First, population pressure on resources is usually attributed to decreased mortality brought about by improved sanitary and health conditions.[2] Although this is true in some cases, what is often overlooked is that the rural population has experienced the fewest improvements in sanitary and health conditions and, consequently, little or less change in mortality than have urban areas. This is apparent in the fact that the two states in Mexico with the highest proportions of their population in the agricultural sector, Chiapas and Oaxaca, have also had the smallest decline in gross mortality rate (from data given in Sanders 1974:16). Relative to the national mortality rate, the situation in such states is worsening. That is, the gap between the more fortunate and the less fortunate is widening. In 1930 the gross mortality rate in Chiapas was below the national average: 20.2 per 1000 in Chiapas compared to 26.6 per 1000 nationally. By 1968 the national rate had dropped to 9.6 per 1000 but, in Chiapas it had dropped only to 12.0. In 1930 the gross mortality rate in Oaxaca was only slightly higher than the national average, 27.5 in Oaxaca compared to 26.6 nationally. By 1968, however, at 14.8 per 1000, Oaxaca's gross mortality rate was 54 percent higher than the national rate. These data suggest that although mortality has been reduced, the reduction has been significantly less in the more rural states.

A comparison of urban and rural growth confirms the picture of slower growth in rural areas. Between 1950 and 1970 the rural population grew at the rate of 35 percent from about 14.8 million to over 20 million. During the same period the urban population increased by 158 percent from 11 million to almost 28.4 million. Some rural growth may be underestimated because a rural locale which passes the 2500 mark is counted as urban, but since the average number of inhabitants in even the largest rural localities (that is, those with 500-2499) was only 966 in 1950 (Cline 1962:103), rural growth is not significantly underestimated. Similarly, some rural growth is alleviated by migration to urban areas. Much of the urban growth is due to this migration, but between 1950 and 1970 the number of Mexicans who migrated from rural to urban areas was only 4.5 million (Lomnitz 1977:43). If they are added to the rural population and subtracted from the urban population (to see what rural growth would be like without migration) the rural population would have grown by 66 percent but the urban population still would have grown by 117 percent. In other words, even without migration the rural population would have grown at only slightly more than half the rate of the urban population.

Despite the fact that rural growth has not been "explosive," the family economy is rapidly declining. Landless rural workers more than doubled from 1.5 million to 3.3 million between 1950 and 1970 and landless workers now compose half of the agricultural workforce (Sanders 1974:5). In other words, the family economy has not been able to absorb even the relatively slow growth of the rural population.

As Table 6 shows, whereas the value of production in a small percent of Mexican farm units (multi-family and large multi-family) has increased significantly, it has risen only slightly in others and declined in the 50 percent of farms below subsistence level. It is this decrease, rather than the population increase, that is destroying the peasant economy.

MEXICAN POLITICAL ECONOMY

Despite the revolution, land reform, and government ownership of some industry, Mexico has pursued the path of capitalist development. This path and its consequent policies have produced an

Table 6
Agricultural Production in Mexico, 1960

TYPE OF HOLDING (BY VALUE OF 1960 PRODUCTION)	PERCENTAGE OF HOLDINGS	VALUE OF PRODUCTION (PERCENTAGE OF TOTAL)	CHANGE OF VALUE OF PRODUCTION 1950–1960 (PERCENTAGE OF TOTAL)
Below subsistence $0–80 (US)	50.3	4.2	−1.0
Subsistence $80–400	33.8	17.1	+10.0
Family $400–2,000	12.6	24.4	+11.0
Multi-Family $2,000–8,000	2.8	22.0	+35.0
Large multi-family above $8,000	.5	32.3	+45.0
Total	100.0	100.0	100.0

Source: Eckstein (1969) cited by Hansen (1971:80).

economic development that has differentially distributed the gains of increased wealth. According to a report made by the United Nations Economic Development Commission for Latin America, in the early 1960s the degree of economic inequality in Mexico was greater than that of most Latin American countries. More recent analysis suggests that, contrary to the view of those who argued that the benefits would "trickle down," relative inequalities have continued to increase. By 1975 the income share of the poorest 50 percent of Mexican families was less than it had been in 1950: 14 percent compared to 19 percent (van Ginnekan 1979:332).

The fact that the poorest segment of the Mexican population has not benefitted from the Mexican "miracle," but rather has suffered from it, has been traced by a number of economists and political scientists to the Mexican state and its policies since 1940.[3] The state, which at times initiates and at times merely supports development efforts, has consistently favored the upper class. As Hansen suggests, "no other Latin American political system has provided more rewards for its new industrial and commercial agricultural elites" (1971:87). The peasant sector has not only been neglected, but peasants have been hurt by government policies favoring both private industry and large-scale capitalist agriculture.

Since 1940 the Mexican state has given industrialization its highest priority. Industrialization has been favored in direct public investment—close to 30 percent of all public investment since 1940 has been in the industrial sector (Hansen 1971:45)—and public policies have encouraged private (both national and foreign) investment in industry. Such policies include protective tariffs, licensing agreements, credit, import privileges, tax concessions, and a fiscal policy favoring price increases and inflation rather than taxes. Industrialists have also benefitted from government policies controlling wages and labor activity. Wages have been kept down by legislation that allows the state to declare strikes illegal and gives it the right to arbitrate any fight (Leal 1975). Most unionized workers are incorporated into the labor sector of PRI (Partido Revolucionario Institucional), the official party, and further controlled by the party.[4]

The advantages given to capitalist industry, both national and foreign, have led to enormous increases in productivity and large profits. In the agricultural sector, however, productivity is significantly lower—only one-sixth of that of the rest of the economy (Hansen 1971:77); for the majority of those in the agricultural sector, productivity is even lower.

The Mexican ruling class has not only favored capitalist industrialization and industrial investment over agriculture and agricultural investment, but the agricultural strategy followed has also favored the rich. Since 1940 the Mexican government has followed a dual agricultural policy which created and maintains two sectors: 1) a small privileged capitalist sector that produces mostly for export and generates most of the marketed agricultural production; and 2) a large sector of poor peasants who live close to the subsistence level (Bartra 1974). Government policies related to the distribution of land, credit, modern technology and the market have increased the productivity and profits of the capitalist sector and decreased the viability of the peasant sector.

Table 7
Irrigation in Mexico

TYPE OF HOLDING (BY VALUE OF 1960 PRODUCTION)	PERCENTAGE OF HOLDINGS	PERCENTAGE OF IRRIGATED LAND
Below subsistence $0–$80	50.3	—
Subsistence $80–$400	33.8	3.9
Family $400–$2000	12.6	27.0
Multi-family $2,000–$8,000	2.8	31.5
Large multi-family above $8,000	.5	37.6
Total	100.0	100.0

Source: Eckstein (1969) cited by Hansen (1971:80).

The Unequal Distribution of Agricultural Inputs

Land reform was an important objective of the Mexican Revolution. Despite the land reform program, property is still very concentrated in a few large landholdings and land concentration is increasing rather than decreasing (Niblo 1975:112). In 1960 half of the landholders, including *ejidatarios* (recipients of land under the Agrarian Reform Program), controlled less than 12 percent of the cropland (Hansen 1971:79). There are still millions of hectares in holdings that violate the agrarian statutes (Hansen 1971:83). Even more problematic is the skewed distribution of other agricultural inputs.

Most of the public money invested in agriculture has been spent on the construction of large irrigation works (Hansen 1971:44). As indicated in Table 7, the land which has been irrigated, including publicly as well as privately financed projects, has been primarily land in large holdings.

Even conservative observers agree that technological change in agriculture has been confined to a small minority of the population.[5] One such technological change was the "Green Revolution." With the help of the Rockefeller Foundation, the Mexican government introduced improved seeds, fertilizer, machinery, and insecticides in the 1950s. However, the new high-yielding seeds could only work under optimum conditions with irrigation and fertilization which were not available to the peasants. The program, supposedly designed to increase the productivity of all cultivators, helped only the large landholders and, in some cases, increased costs and decreased productivity among peasants.[6] Another program, Plan Puebla, also supported by the Rockefeller Foundation (Edelman 1980:33) was designed specifically for small-scale farmers dependent on rainfall and traditional technology. It encouraged cultivators to change their fertilizer use patterns and the timing and spacing of plant populations. As one supporter of the plan notes however, after seven years the plan had not met expectations and increased yields to their full potential (Sanders 1974b:13). According to another study, the plan's recommendations had a negative effect on corn yields (Gladwin 1979:665).[7] Still another attempt, Plan Zacapoaxtla, also in Puebla, benefitted a few of the better off landowners and pushed others off the land completely. Those with less or no land who had formerly rented land were priced off the land as rents rose (Edelman 1980:42).

The major reasons for the failure of Plan Puebla and similar programs are: 1) they rarely have sufficient resources to provide the technical information to those who are supposed to benefit, and 2) they do not provide sufficient credit to enable the target populations to participate in the new more expensive procedures. Gladwin (1979) found that many people had misinformation about these procedures. In another community, ten years after the initiation of Plan Puebla, most of the target population received fertilizer one month after sowing, too late to do any good (Turrent cited by Redclift 1980:499). These two problems are part of the general neglect of peasant agriculture. Extension services have been minimal. Hansen points out that the proportion of extension agents to farm families, approximately one to ten thousand, is lower than most other Central American republics (Hansen 1971:86). Even after recent unprecedented investment in agricultural education in the early 1970s, less than one-fifth of the rural population were receiving full extension services (Sanders 1975:15).

Rural credit has also been denied peasants except at high rates from private moneylenders. Agricultural credit from the government and banking institutions has gone primarily to the private commercial-farm sector rather than the ejido (land reform) sector (de Janvry and Ground 1978:104). Ejidatarios cannot get credit from the private sector because they do not own their land. Nor is there much credit available from the government. Between 1936 and 1960 the proportion of ejidatarios who received credit from the government fell from 30 to 14 percent (Hansen 1971:82). In 1975 the government increased the amount of credit available to the agricultural sector, but even with the increase, only 20 percent of the needed agricultural credit is supplied by the government. (Niblo 1975:123). Furthermore, since the new government credit goes only to the peasants who have the training to use it properly, it goes to those who already have the greatest access to other agricultural inputs (Niblo 1975:123). As indicated in the study by Edelman of Plan Zacapoaxtla described above, this polarization results not only in some not benefitting, but in a deterioration of conditions for the less fortunate since the land they formerly rented can be put to more profitable use by those who have access to credit.

A final factor that contributes to the adverse position of peasants is the disadvantage they face in the capitalist market.[8] Not only have peasants lost access to land because the price of rented or purchased land rises as those with more capital can produce more, but they are also forced to sell at reduced prices. Market prices, including the official prices set by the government, are determined primarily by the large capitalist enterprises. The low productivity of peasant production, which is a consequence of poor lands, primitive technology, and high transportation costs caused by lack of access to markets, means that if peasant labor is included, the production costs of peasants are higher than those of capitalist agriculture. Thus, peasants sell at a loss.[9] Although peasants, as Chayanov (1966) suggests, may not calculate the costs of family labor, they cannot help but notice that they are working more and receiving less. That they are receiving less is apparent in the assessment made in 1975 by Dr. Adolfo Chavez, chief of the Division of Nutrition of the National Institute of Nutrition, that in the four previous years peasants had to reduce their average caloric intake by 20 percent (Niblo 1975:118). Peasants are also more directly exploited by middlemen to whom they are indebted for credit and forced to sell their products at prices determined by the middlemen. Anderson Clayton, a U.S. transnational which began in the cotton business and is today an international oilseed producer, coffee merchant, and consumer food concern with 40 percent of its total operations in Mexico and Brazil (*New York Times*, November 28, 1980:D4), gives more credit for cotton production than the National Ejido Bank gives to all ejidatarios (Barkin 1975:72). Anderson Clayton's manipulation of credit is an important mechanism in controlling the market.

Insufficient land is only part of the peasant's problem. Credit and modern technology are also lacking in the peasant sector. But, in the capitalist sector, credit, modern technology, and more fertile land are not lacking. Not only has the Mexican state not supported peasant agriculture but, by promoting the development of capitalist agriculture and capitalist industrialization, the state has promoted a process which destroys the peasant economy. Peasants must become pauperized and/or proletarianized.

As in the rest of Mexico, even in the densely settled region in which San Cosme is located, the decline of the family economy and depeasantization are occurring only partly because of lack of land and rapid population growth. As indicated in Chapter 1, rapid population growth is a recent phenomenon in San Cosme and came as the result of the proletarianization of a large proportion of the community's population.

SMALL-SCALE CULTIVATION IN SAN COSME

Ninety-five percent of the properties in the state of Tlaxcala are less than five hectares. The other 5 percent occupy 75 percent of the area (calculated from data in Banco de Comercio 1970:49). Almost all San Cosmeros are among the 95 percent of the Tlaxcaltecans who have less than five hectares. The few who have more, about five families with fifteen hectares each, will shortly have to subdivide among their children.

All San Cosmeros primarily practice traditional agriculture with primitive technology. Because of its location in a semi-arid, sub-humid zone and because only a small proportion of San Cosmeros have access to irrigation, agriculture is temporal. Plow culture predominates and corn is the principal and sometimes the only crop planted. Other vegetables, such as beans and squash, may be interspersed with the corn and most families have a garden with nut, avocado, or fruit trees.

For everybody in the community the possibilities of changing the methods and/or crops and improving productivity are extremely limited. Some people have tried to increase their agricultural productivity, but this often requires extra cash for investment in new or additional agricultural inputs, so it is usually only the proletarians who can afford to experiment. Often the experiments are relatively costly and unsuccessful. What follows are a few examples of the attempts San Cosmeros have made to increase productivity; they are typical of the difficulties encountered.

In 1971 a state agricultural expert, following Plan Puebla, recommended the use of two applications of a new fertilizer. Government credit was available to pay for the fertilizer at an interest rate of 1 percent a month. A number of obreros were able to make the necessary investment. The peasants, however, were reluctant to take the risk without knowing for sure that it would pay off. The money for fertilizer was to be loaned by the state in March, before planting, and had to be paid back the following February. While this allowed them to harvest the crops in October before paying back the loan, since the highest prices for corn are in the summer, before the harvest, many would have had to sell earlier and at lower prices in order to pay back their loans. Most of the thirty San Cosmeros who decided to experiment were factory workers or merchants. The results have been inconsistent. Some of the original thirty, plus others, continue using the two applications. Others decided that the extra costs in fertilizer and labor were too great for the small and uncertain return.

Many San Cosmeros have also tried to raise pigs, chickens, and cows. Some succeed but they need not only the cash for the initial investment but the financial flexibility to suffer animal losses as well. For example, one peasant family tried to raise pigs. In addition to the initial investment in two pigs, after the piglets were born, the mother pig could not nurse them. The family borrowed money so that they could buy milk (which the family could never afford to drink themselves) for the piglets. The piglets and the mother pig died anyway. The woman said she would never try to raise pigs again. Another effort to raise animals was sponsored by the state government. An extension agent came to San Cosme and announced that the state was selling hens. She first had to inspect the facilities that families had to raise chickens. Four women from San Cosme, who had received approval for their facilities, went to buy the hens. On the two-hour bus trip back to San Cosme, 25 of the 100 hens they purchased died of suffocation. It is usually only those San Cosmeros with a regular non-agricultural source of income who can afford the extra costs and risks involved in new agricultural efforts.

Because of the community's accessibility to Mexico City and Puebla, San Cosmeros have greater access to markets than many Mexican peasants. San Cosmeros frequently sell their corn above the official government price. During the summer of 1980, for example, corn was being sold in San Cosme for seven pesos a kilo. In another, more remote community in Tlaxcala, where access to markets was less, it was selling at four and a half pesos a kilo.

The ability to sell corn at a higher price also varies within the community. The precarious economic position of peasants puts them in a more disadvantaged position than the obreros. Proletarians may hold off selling their corn until the price rises or until they find a buyer willing to pay a higher price. Peasants, on the other hand, often have to sell immediately after the harvest, when prices are their lowest, or in an emergency to meet some necessary expense. Thus, even in San Cosme where access to markets is greater, peasants are constrained by their poverty from getting higher prices for their produce.

To aggravate the situation, negotiations are currently underway for the purchase of a large area of San Cosme's cultivated land for factories. Not only do capitalist industrialists have greater financial resources and greater potential productivity which place peasants at a disadvantage in the competition for land, but they have government support as well. San Cosmeros have been told by the local politicians that if they do not sell the land to the industrialists, the land will be expropriated.

CONCLUSION

For as long as they can remember San Cosmeros have supplemented subsistence cultivation with a variety of economic activities. Peasant men, women, and children worked in the fields of others, sold wood or pulque, or engaged in some other economic activity to supplement their income from subsistence production. Although the population of San Cosme did not grow rapidly until the late 1960s, even their slow rate of growth could not be absorbed by the peasant economy because few changes had occurred which might have increased peasant productivity. As a consequence of steady or declining productivity, competition from capitalist agriculture and industry, and population growth, San Cosmeros must sell their labor more often. A large proportion of the economically active male population, 60 percent, now work full-time as factory workers. Much of what they earn goes to support peasants and to maintain the peasant economy. Of the seventy-eight households headed by peasants in the author's 1980 census, thirty-two (41 percent) include one or more full-time wage earners. In addition to relying on the wages of other family members who are usually factory workers or domestics, many peasants have increased the number of days they work for wages. In this respect, as well as having at least the possibility of factory work, the peasants of San Cosme differ from less fortunate peasants elsewhere in Mexico. According to one estimate, landless rural laborers have experienced a decline in the number of days they obtain work annually from 194 in 1950 to 75 in 1970 (*Excelsior* cited by Sanders 1975:11). Not only do the peasants of San Cosme have some land, but some additional wage work, compatible with subsistence cultivation, has been generated by proletarianization. Obreros hire campesinos to work in their fields. The income from factory work has stimulated building in the community and created some part-time work for peasant men as masons. Campesinos who supplement their income as musicians seem to be working more often since factory workers can now afford to celebrate such life cycle events as marriage, or the fifteenth birthday of a daughter, with more elaborate fiestas. At the same time, however, the more autonomous supplementary economic activities in which peasants sold a product, such as pulque or wood, are declining. (The demand for wood has decreased because petroleum is cheaper, but peasants cannot afford the cash investment necessary to sell petroleum.) Tractors, usually owned by non-peasants and often non-San Cosmeros, are also replacing the animal-driven plows owned and used by peasants. San Cosmeros thus sell their labor more often and in less autonomous ways than in the past.

Development policy in Mexico has favored industry and large-scale agriculture. Productivity in these sectors has increased significantly. However, peasant productivity has not increased and the peasant economy cannot compete with the more dynamic capitalist economy. Peasants must become poorer and/or proletarianized.

In the family economy, men, women and children are all required to give their labor to produce what the family consumes and sells. The unit and locus of production, reproduction, and consumption is the same: the family farm. Production, reproduction, and consumption are not distinct and hierarchially arranged spheres. With the expansion of industrial capitalism, the productive unit becomes a unit of capital, a firm or enterprise which employs individuals (Sen 1980:83). The physical locus of production shifts from the household to the factory or "factories in the field." Wage work replaces subsistence production and small-scale commodity production. The family continues as a unit of consumption but family consumption depends not on family production but on the ability of individual family members to sell their labor. The labor process in a capitalist society is not a technical process; it is primarily a process of accumulation of capital (Braverman 1975:20). The worker enters into employment because social conditions—the concentration of the means of production—leave him or her no other way to gain a livelihood. The employer, on the other hand, hires labor in order to enlarge his capital (Braverman 1974:53). In order to sell their labor, therefore, San Cosmeros must fit into the scheme of things as determined by the logic of capitalism, which is the maximization of profit.

NOTES

1. Lewis similarly found that births in Tepoztlan were often recorded in years other than the one in which they occurred (1963:32).

2. See Cline (1963:85) and Sanders (1974:6).

3. For discussions of the relation between these policies and capitalism and imperialism see Leal (1975) and Baird and McCaughan (1979:71–117).

4. See Chapter 5 for a discussion of such control of the factory workers from San Cosme.

5. See, for example, Sanders (1975:3).

6. See Hewitt de Alcantara (1974).

7. For a discussion of the political considerations, including land invasions by peasants which influenced the development of Plan Puebla, see Paré (1975).

8. See Bartra (1974) for a comprehensive discussion of peasants and the capitalist market.

9. Craft production is similarly affected by competition from the capitalist market.

4

The Private World of Proletarian Women

In the family economy women are more likely to do the work at the processing end of the continuum but are not exclusively confined to processing and childcare. As capitalist industrialization has developed in Mexico, women in San Cosme have become less involved in production and their world has become increasingly focused on domestic activities. It is a world that is separate from, but dependent on, the work world of men. Even the designation proletarian women derives, for most women, not from their own economic activity but from the factory work of their husbands or fathers, because proletarianization has meant withdrawal of women from production.

THE RETREAT FROM PRODUCTION

Proletarian women's lesser involvement in production is twofold. First, they are not usually wage workers in the capitalist sector. And second, their involvement in subsistence production in the noncapitalist sector has become less significant both absolutely and relatively.

With the expansion of industrial capitalism and proletarianization, three significant changes occur which influence the participation of women in production and ultimately, their general position in society. First, in a capitalist system, workers own no means of production, or, as in the case of rural Mexico, insufficient and unproductive means of production, other than their own labor, so they are dependent on the sale of their labor.

Second, with the concentration of production in enterprises or firms, production, reproduction and consumption become differentiated both spatially and socially. Production takes place outside the home in what becomes the more prestigious public sphere and reproduction and consumption become the functions of the less prestigious private or domestic sphere. A third characteristic of industrial capitalism is that the labor process comes under the control of the capitalist and is dominated by the pursuit of profit. In a capitalist system, therefore, labor must be sold physically away from the home and those who buy labor power determine not only where one works but who can work and when. In this system woman's childbearing ability becomes an obstacle to production (Sen 1980:82).

Recent cross-cultural studies have shown an enormous variation in the roles and status of women. These studies also show that although women have the main responsibility for children and domestic tasks in all societies, until recently such tasks were combined with important productive activities. This is apparent in the family economy discussed earlier. Studies of gathering-hunting and horticultural societies similarly show that women combined production, reproduction, and consumption.[1] Under the work conditions of industrial capitalism, however, the interweaving of reproductive, consumptive, and productive activities is more difficult (Deere 1979 and Sen 1980). Not only are work and home separated, but wage work has a rigid time structure. Except in the lowest paying and least stable jobs, where intermittent participation and a temporary labor force is to the advantage of capitalists, the interruptions of childbearing and childcare are extra costs for capitalists to avoid.[2]

Mexican capitalists, like capitalists elsewhere, avoid these and other extra costs entailed by protective legislation by not hiring women or by hiring only young, unmarried women whom medical examinations have shown are not pregnant. This is reflected in the lack of job opportunities for the women of San Cosme. The factory jobs available to the men are not open to the women. Some young women are obreras but the "women's factories" in which they work and which primarily hire women will not hire those over the age of twenty-five or thirty. Some women are maids in Mexico City or

Puebla; a few with specialized training are nurses or teachers, but very few women have such training. Given their limited choices most women in San Cosme, if they are not peasants, are homemakers (*amas de la casa*).

Although most women in San Cosme do not work for wages, proletarian women do contribute to their family's economic support. Proletarian women still participate in the subsistence sector but because this is the less productive, noncapitalist sphere, it is not highly valued and, like the family economy, is declining.

Proletarian women contribute economically by raising chickens, cows, and pigs for family consumption and, to a lesser extent, for sale. They also work in the fields and gardens and many women sew for their own families and for others. In families with stores, women work in the store. A few women work part-time as auxiliary nurses or midwives. Nursing, sewing, and dispatching in a store all require either specialized training and/or a significant financial investment which most women do not have. Consequently, the major economic contributions of proletarian women are in agriculture. The spot observations of proletarian families indicate that proletarian women were engaged in productive activities in 23 percent of the observations; of these two-thirds were agricultural activities and one-third were non-agricultural economic activities.

The small-scale cultivation practiced by San Cosmeros is not very profitable, yet in peasant families, despite its unprofitability, it still represents the main source of the family's consumption. In proletarian families, however, what they themselves produce and what they can buy with the proceeds of small-scale cultivation represents a very small share of the family's consumption. For example, in 1979 one proletarian family, with more land than the average, used 1500 kilos of corn (for themselves and to feed their animals) and sold about 3000 kilos. The value of their production, using the official price of corn and not counting the costs involved, was a little more than 20,000 pesos. Compared to the family's income from wages of about 80,000 pesos, small-scale cultivation represents only about one-fourth of their income. As the profitability of small-scale production continues to decline, its relative contribution to consumption also declines. As a result, many proletarian families have reduced their level of agricultural

Proletarian Woman Doing Piecework at Home. *Photograph by the author.*

activity. Most proletarian families still plant enough corn for their families but they are less likely to plant other products, such as squash or beans, and they weed and check their fields less frequently. The long walk to the fields, the arduousness of the work, and its low return discourage many people from doing any but the most necessary tasks of planting, fertilizing, occasional weeding, and harvesting.

Among proletarian women two patterns have emerged in response to the declining significance of subsistence cultivation. Some women have withdrawn almost completely from subsistence production. They may raise chickens and vegetables in gardens near the house but they do not go out to the fields. Other women have continued to play an important role in subsistence cultivation. They may even be doing more subsistence production than peasant women because they take over some of the tasks men or children would do in peasant families, but because the family farm is less significant for family consumption, their work is not highly valued. In some cases subsistence production or small-scale commodity production, such as cutting and selling wood, which proletarian women usually do not do because the returns are very low, may be done temporarily by a woman while her husband is unemployed and looking for a job. For example, while the husband was unemployed for a year, the wife of an obrero cooked and sold foods, such as tamales, at local fiestas. The devaluation of women's subsistence production is reflected in the growing belief among San Cosmeros that it is more modern for women to stay home and take care of their houses and families rather than go to the fields.

In sum, most proletarian women are neither involved in the capitalist sector of wage work nor seen as contributing a significant share via their participation in the noncapitalist sector. Even those women who still do agricultural work are not viewed as making a significant economic contribution because their production represents only a small part of the family's consumption. Capitalist industrialization and proletarianization have thus redefined the role of women in San Cosme. They have been driven out of subsistence production by competition from the more productive capitalist sector, but they are excluded from the world of industrial wage labor.

THE DOMESTIC WORLD OF PROLETARIAN WOMEN

As their productive role diminishes, the domain of proletarian women has increasingly become confined to the domestic or private sphere. An examination of their domestic activities suggests moreover that this world is not merely different but isolated from and dependent on the men's public world of work and politics.

As indicated in Chapter 2, in the peasant family the greater responsibility of women for domestic tasks did not mean other family members did not share that responsibility. In proletarian families, however, adult women are more likely to bear the burden of domestic activities alone. It is not merely a physical isolation but a social isolation as well. The major difference between peasant and proletarian families is greater involvement of peasant daughters in domestic activities (see Table 8). The spot observations indicate that females did more than 80 percent of the domestic tasks recorded in both peasant and proletarian families. Among peasants, mothers did less than half of the domestic work; among proletarians, mothers did more than half of the domestic tasks. This accounts for the greater likelihood of proletarian mothers being alone (see Table 9).

Given their greater responsibility for domestic work and their lesser involvement in production, it is not surprising that socially, proletarian women are more isolated. In peasant families the roles of all family members are more likely to overlap; in proletarian families roles are more specialized (see Table 10). However, whereas the specialized roles of proletarian men and children take them out of the home, the specialized roles of proletarian women confine them to the home.

Most of the obreros are active in local politics and when he is not working in the factory a proletarian man is likely to be interacting with local or visiting politicians or socializing with other men of the community at one of the stores that serves beer and liquor. The activities of the proletarian men take them outside the community or to public places in the community—the municipal offices or stores. The proletarian woman, on the other hand, interacts in small groups in her own home or the home of a relative or neighbor. The main public interaction for proletarian women is in

Table 8
Division of Domestic Labor in San Cosme

	NUMBER OF OCCASIONS DOMESTIC ACTIVITIES OBSERVED*	PERCENTAGE
Proletarian		
Families		
Mothers	54	61.2
Daughters	18	20.5
Sons	10	11.4
Fathers	6	6.9
Total	88	100.0
Peasant		
Families		
Mothers	30	46.9
Daughters	22	34.4
Sons	8	12.5
Fathers	4	6.3
Total	64	100.1

Source: Spot observations of eight peasant and fifteen proletarian families.

Note: The percentage total under "Peasant Families" exceeds 100 due to rounding.

*Domestic activities include: food processing, sewing, washing, housecleaning and repair, shopping, and child care when it is the sole activity.

Table 9
Social Isolation of Mothers in San Cosme

	OBSERVED ALONE		OBSERVED WITH OTHERS		TOTAL OBSERVATIONS	
	No.	%	No.	%	No.	%
Peasant Mothers	22	33.9	43	66.2	65	100.1
Proletarian Mothers	49	40.5	72	59.5	121	100.0

Source: Spot observations of eight peasant and fifteen proletarian families.

Note: The percentage total under "Peasant Mothers" exceeds 100 due to rounding.

Table 10
Role Overlap in San Cosme

NUMBER OF ACTIVITIES*	PEASANT FAMILIES	FACTORY WORKER FAMILIES
Overlap between Spouses		
0	—	4
1	3	5
2	3	5
3	2	1
Total	8	15
Overlap between Mothers and Children		
0	—	1
1	—	4
2	5	8
3	3	2
Total	8	15
Overlap between Fathers and Children		
0	—	1
1	—	2
2	5	7
3	3	5
Total	8	15

Source: Spot observations of eight peasant and fifteen proletarian families.

*The activities are: wage work or commercial activities, agriculture, and domestic activities.

the morning when they go to the mill. Proletarian women, but not peasant women, are criticized by their husbands and other San Cosmeros if they leave San Cosme too frequently alone. The wife of one worker said: "Men can leave and go where they want. Women have to stay home like *ratones* [rats]."

The difference in spheres for proletarian men and women is very apparent in the two different worlds of one couple. The husband works in nearby Puebla and has a motorcycle, but he stays in

Puebla and returns to San Cosme only on weekends, primarily to participate in local politics. In Puebla he lives with a young woman. His wife stays in San Cosme and rarely leaves the community except to go to a nearby community for medical care for herself or one of the children. When referring to his wife and her narrower sphere, the husband often says, "She has her chickens." Although she is one of the largest chicken raisers in San Cosme, this activity occurs almost completely within the confines of her front yard; she buys them from a vendor who comes to San Cosme, she raises them in her yard, and she sells them from her yard.

Unlike the proletariat, the peasants do not have distinct spheres for men and women. As mentioned in Chapter 2, their economic contribution is relatively equal. It is similar in nature as well as quantity. Circumstances such as where they interact and with whom they interact are much more likely to overlap. The activities of the peasant woman take her to the same locale as her husband—the fields, the mountain, or the local streets if she is selling flowers or wood. Neither the peasant woman nor the peasant man spends much time socializing in the stores nor do they spend time outside the community.

Factory workers, by the nature of their activities, interact with a more diverse group of people. They interact with people from other communities as well as fellow San Cosmeros, with urbanites as well as rural people, Mestizo as well as Indian, professionals as well as peasants and workers. Sometimes a proletarian woman will meet these people but it is through her husband and she usually only says hello and then goes back to the kitchen, her own or someone else's. Even when the activities of the proletarian man and woman overlap, as in their involvement with education, there is a differentiation within the activity. The men interact with visiting officials or go to state and national offices to solicit funds, while proletarian women continue to perform the domestic chores connected with the visits. For example, at the end of the first year of San Cosme's new secondary school, the students put on a performance to which the district supervisor, a man from Puebla, was invited. After the performance, the head of the parents' committee, a factory worker, invited the district head, the district head's family, the teacher, about fifteen local politicians, and the anthropologist to his house for mole. The wives and daughters of the men of the parents' committee were there but came out of the kitchen only to serve.

The domestic world of proletarian women is not only differentiated and isolated from the public world of men—it is also subordinate to it. The private world of the family is subject to the political decisions made in the largely male public world (see Chapter 5) and proletarian women are economically dependent on men to support their domestic activities.

The spot observations indicate that the overall level of domestic activity is the same for proletarian and peasant women. Both proletarian and peasant women were found to be engaged in domestic activities (food processing, sweeping, sewing, washing, shopping, and childcare) in 44 percent of the observations.[3] The kind of domestic activity which predominates, however, is different. More than 50 percent of the domestic activities of peasant women consisted of cooking or other food processing. Among proletarian women, food processing accounted for only a third of their domestic tasks. The time spent on food processing has been reduced in proletarian homes by the use of gas stoves and petroleum fires rather than wood fires, and by the greater consumption among proletarians of purchased foods such as bread; yet proletarian women are more likely to cook a greater number of meals, with more variety. Their higher income enables them to have *atole* (a hot drink made of corn or rice flour) for breakfast, often with rolls, a dinner of eggs, meat, or vegetables, and a light supper of leftovers or *chalupas, elotes,* or *tacos.* The peasant woman is more likely to make a big pot of beans and the family eats beans and tortillas for its main meal and then again for breakfast the next day. Because proletarian children are more likely to go to school (see Chapter 6) and the factory worker's schedule varies from the school day, the proletarian woman not only makes more diverse meals but also serves meals more frequently. One proletarian woman, for example, serves breakfast at 8:00 A.M. to the whole family. At noon she serves lunch to her husband before he leaves for work at 1:00 P.M. She eats dinner with her children when they get home from school at 2:00 P.M. In the evening, she and the children have a light supper and at midnight she reheats dinner for

Proletarian *Woman Husking Corn for Dinner.* She did not accompany the family to the fields and this was the only time the family ate elotes. The trip to the fields was made because the children wanted to eat elotes. *Photograph by the author.*

her husband. Although the more diverse diet and diverse family activities make for additional and more complicated meals, the proletarian woman spends less time preparing them because of the greater use of gas stoves and the greater consumption of store-bought items such as bread and canned sardines.

Although proletarian women spend less time cooking, they spend more time shopping and washing. That is, they spend more time buying and maintaining the larger stock of consumption goods, such as clothes and bed linen. They have replaced production with consumption. As Galbraith notes about women in the United States:

> The administration of consumption resides with the woman. This involves much choice as to purchases. . . . The conventional wisdom celebrates this power; it is women who hold the purse strings. In fact this is normally the power to implement decisions, not to make them. Action, within the larger strategic framework, is established by the man who provides the money. The household . . . is essentially a disguise for the exercise of male authority. (1973:35–36).

In order to practice her tasks of consumption, the proletarian woman in San Cosme is now dependent on her husband. Proletarian men control the greater share of the family's income and give their wives a household allowance. In one case, a factory worker gives his wife five hundred of the thirteen hundred pesos he earns a week. From this she pays for food not produced by the family (sugar, salt, candy, fruit, onions, chiles, meat, bread, milk, potatoes, and beans), clothes for herself and their four children, school expenses, electricity, water, medication, and gas. He uses the remainder to cover his transportation and living expenses in Mexico City and for large purchases such as land, a stove, a television, or a car.

Proletarian women sometimes sell small quantities of corn and use the money as they wish, but larger quantities are sold by the men. The proletarian woman controls her earnings from sewing or selling chickens, but these are relatively small amounts and she is usually dependent on the husband for the initial investment in a sewing machine or animals. Major decisions, such as whether a child should go to secondary school or whether the family should buy a gas stove or television, are made by the men. Women can try to influence decisions by making life difficult for their husbands, by being unpleasant or irresponsible, but then the husband might get another wife. The proletarian wife cannot leave her husband without suffering a decline in her standard of living by becoming a peasant or paid domestic. In one case, for example, a woman left her husband because he had a girl friend. After leaving her children with her mother and working as a maid in Mexico City for a few years, she decided to go back with her husband even though he spent most of his time with the other woman. Women sometimes have extramartial affairs but they are criticized for doing so, and a woman is ostracized if she leaves her husband for another man.

As production is removed from the home and the family and women are removed from production, their tasks become those of consumption and reproduction. Although the authority of proletarian husbands is increasingly felt, proletarian women in San Cosme are not regarded as "just housewives," the expression used in the United States and other advanced capitalist countries to indicate a social devalutaion of the homemaker role. Neither the women nor the men of San Cosme consider the domestic work of women or women themselves as less important. Both men and women think that men are physically stronger and have greater sexual desires; other abilities, however, including intellectual ability and emotional and physical health, are seen to vary individually, not by sex. When, for example, a woman was elected president of San Cosme, many people objected to her on the basis that she favored certain segments ofthe community over others or because she was a manipulator, but the only person who disparaged her for being a woman was a man from the neighboring and more proletarianized community of Papalotla.

Although there are two different worlds, a woman's world of domesticity and a man's world of factory work and politics, neither world is yet ranked more important or more demanding of special characteristics and abilities. The native model does not yet relegate the different spheres of proletarian women and men to different ranks.

As Beechey suggests, however, the relationship between production, reproduction, and consumption changes historically (1978:194). The potential for greater inequities has been laid in the greater economic power of the men and their control of the public sphere. Although it is impossible to predict all that will happen in the future, there are hints that the relationship is beginning to change. As the labor process demands more education, children and childhood become more expensive (see Chapter 6). Elsewhere, this process has often led older women into the work force.[4] Then the different world of women, their domesticity, serves as the basis for the devaluation of women and their work and rationalizes hiring women at lower wages and in less stable jobs. This in turn unites them with other segments of the population.

Mexico already has a very high rate of unemployment. In addition to the entry of proletarian women into the work force, depeasantization will continue to add millions of job seekers. The next chapter will examine those who have jobs, the obreros. Later chapters will consider whether it is likely that the gap between proletarian women and men will continue to increase or whether the benefits gained by the men from the Mexican "miracle" are themselves only temporary.

NOTES

1. See Leacock (1981) and Boserup (1970).
2. See Sokoloff (1980) and Ehrenreich and Fuentes (1981) for discussions of situations in which employing women in low-paying and temporary jobs is to the advantage of capitalists.
3. During the months of heightened agricultural activity, October when they harvest and March when they plant, peasant women probably do less domestic work. Since the period of greater agricultural activity is short, however, the observations made in August and September are probably representative of most of the year.
4. See Safa (1978).

CHAPTER

5

The Public World of Proletarian Men

The purpose of this chapter is twofold. First, it will describe the world of San Cosme's obreros and compare it to the lives of their wives and peasant neighbors. Second, it will situate that world in its larger class context. As Braverman suggests:

> The complexities of the class structure of pre-monopoly capitalism arose from the fact that so large a proportion of the working population, being neither employed by capital nor itself employing labor to any significant extent, fell outside the capital-labor polarity. The complexity of the class structure of modern monopoly capitalism arises from the very opposite consideration: namely, that *almost all of the population has been transformed into employees of capital.* (1974:404, stress in the original)

The factory workers of San Cosme, as employees of capital, are subject to and subjects in the class process generated by capitalism's drive for accumulation. The first part of this chapter, which describes the world of factory workers, is akin to stopping history. As Thompson notes:

> If we stop history at a given point, then there are no classes but simply a multitude of individuals with a multitude of experiences. But if we watch these men over an adequate period of social change, we observe patterns in their relation-

ships, their ideas and their institutions. Class is defined by men as they live their own history, and in the end, this is its only definition. (1966:11)

The second part of this chapter examines the dynamic relationship between obreros and capital over the past forty years.

THE WORK WORLD

As indicated in Table 11, factory work is the principal occupation of 48 percent of the men over twelve. Although a few young women work in factories and a few men and women have non-factory employment in the capitalist sector, the largest concentration of workers is male factory workers.

Most of San Cosme's obreros work in textile factories as *coneros* or *trocileros* (semi-skilled operators of textile machines). Usually they work in the same factory as other San Cosmeros. More than half of all the factory workers in the author's census work in one of four factories, Agua Azul and Abetex in Puebla and Magicos and Ilmex in Mexico City. Although San Cosme is located only a few miles from the Puebla-Tlaxcala industrial corridor, most San Cosmeros do not work in factories in the corridor. Some of the newer

Table 11
Principal Occupation of Males in San Cosme
(twelve and over)

	NUMBER	PERCENTAGE
Factory Worker	159	48.3
Peasant	75	22.8
Student	63	19.1
Other	32	9.7
Total	329	99.9

Source: Author's census, 1980.

factories there, including several transnationals such as Resistol (a division of Monsanto which produces polystyrene) and Moto Equipos (a part of Rolls Royce which makes industrial engines), require more education or skill than most of the San Cosmeros have. Other factories along the corridor are controlled by workers from other communities and it is difficult for San Cosmeros to get jobs there. Consequently, San Cosmeros commute either daily to Puebla or weekly to Mexico City.

The age distribution of those working in Mexico City compared to the age distribution of those working in Puebla (see Table 12), as well as comments made by workers, suggests that young workers go first to Puebla or to one of the two local factories where San Cosmeros work. Then, after they have learned the job, either as an unpaid apprentice or by working as a janitor and learning from one of the other workers (usually a relative), they go to Mexico City where wages are higher and jobs more available. As they get older, they return to a factory in Puebla or they become campesinos in San Cosme.

Until recently, the only requirements for getting a job as a textile worker were knowing someone in the factory and giving a cash gift

Table 12
Location of Factories Where San Cosmeros
Work at Different Ages

AGE	MEXICO CITY		PUEBLA	
	No.	%	No.	%
19 or under	8	32	17	68
20–29	27	75	9	25
30–40	22	65	12	35
40–49	9	39	14	61
50 and above	4	57	3	43

Source: Author's census, 1980.

to the head of the union. Few of the older factory workers have more than two or three years of schooling. Recently, the educational requirements have been increased. New workers are now required to have a certificate from primary school as well as knowing someone and giving a gift to the union leader. Those with more education, including some who have completed secondary school, do the same work as the older, less educated workers unless they have specialized training as mechanics (see Chapter 6). Few San Cosmeros have such training.

Regardless of their education or experience most of the obreros work "por contracto," that is, on temporary three-month or one-year contracts, and are frequently laid off. For this reason, it is not unusual for a factory worker who has worked twenty or thirty years as a textile worker to have worked in a number of different factories and to have spent anywhere from a month to several years between jobs. In the beginning of their careers, when they are learning the machines, they often earn below the minimum wage. Once they become coneros or trocileros they may work on a piece-rate basis. Most earn the minimum wage or slightly more and receive wage increases according to the minimum wages set by the Comision Nacional de los Salarios Minimos (the government minimum wage commission).

Unless they are working the night shift, they work eight hours a day, six days a week. If, as happens often now with the more modern machines that are being imported from Germany and other countries, their machine breaks down, a mechanic must be called and while they are waiting they cannot work and are not paid. Similarly, when factories were closed in 1980 for several hours a day to conserve electricity, the obreros were not paid.

Thus, the work world of the obreros is one of long hours, low pay, insecurity, and no vertical mobility. More and more, as their factories modernize with more advanced technology, they cannot fix their own machines as they used to, and they are further removed from control and knowledge of the production process.

For the majority who work in Mexico City, factory work also means living in a rented room with three or four other workers, buying meals (usually from a woman who cooks for a number of factory workers), and returning to San Cosme only on the weekends. Some of the obreros have moved permanently to Mexico City but most say it is too expensive and it is better for their families to live in San Cosme. Some men have mistresses or girl friends in Mexico City and do not return weekly. Most, however, go to Mexico City (or Puebla) just to work; their non-work lives revolve around San Cosme and, despite their absence, they dominate the community.

Most of the obreros have families and land in San Cosme and they participate in the political, and to a lesser extent, the religious systems of the community. Each week buses of factory workers come and go directly between San Cosme and Mexico City. Even after they leave, late Sunday night or Monday morning, the influence of the workers and their factory work is very apparent.

FACTORY WORK AND POLITICS:
PATRON-CLIENT RELATIONS

That San Cosmeros get jobs by knowing somebody and making a gift, formerly of cash and now a bottle of liquor, is only one part of a complicated hierarchical system of patron-client relations that dominates not just the factory but what Bartra (1975) calls "the structure of mediation" as well. In order to see the complete scope of the oberos' world, it is necessary to consider the Mexican political system, the place of the obreros in that system, and the obreros in San Cosme politics.

The Mexican Political System: Centralization of Power

Most observers of the Mexican political system are in substantial agreement that the national president dominates the entire system. Even writers such as Scott, who see the president as being influenced by a variety of interest groups, recognize that the ultimate core of power resides in the president (1959:32). Directly or indirectly, the president controls public policy, appointment to political and administrative positions, and adjudication.

The three important levels of government in Mexico are the federal government, the state, and the free municipio. At each of these levels there are three arms—the government, the Partido Revolucionario Institucional (PRI), and the various sectors of the PRI. Opposition parties could be additional vertical systems. In most states, however, including Tlaxcala, opposition parties are insignificant, if they exist at all. The chances for the existence and success of opposition parties is limited by the system. The national law regarding political parties enhances the position of the PRI. The law, in addition to establishing difficult requirements for political parties, is administered by the central government's Secretaria de Gobernacion (Scott 1959:147-148). This agency, not surprisingly, exhibits a bias in favor of the PRI. This is apparent in the recognition that they grant to some opposition parties as opposed to others. According to Scott, the Partido Autentico de la Revolucion Mexicana (PARM) was granted recognition before the 1958 presidential election despite its doubtful ability to meet the membership requirements of the law, and recognition of the stronger and better organized communist party was refused (1959:148). Even observers such as Needler, who are unwilling to accept the idea that the Mexican elections are fraudulent by national design, admits that the national leadership might annul an election won by the opposition and concedes that some overenthusiastic PRI partisans may have done so in the 1968 municipal election in Tijuana (1971:15).

Within the party and the government, presidential control is maintained through a variety of mechanisms, the main one being the PRI. Since its inception in 1929, PRI has always held the presidency and most other posts, including state governorships, federal senatorial posts, and mayoralities. Given the great likelihood that PRI candidates will win, the selection process for candidates of the official party is very important.

Theoretically, PRI candidates for municipal, state, and national offices are selected at PRI nominating conventions. A great deal of evidence indicates that in actuality these conventions, acting on instructions from the Central Executive Committee of the PRI, nominate the choices made directly or indirectly by the president.

The president does not directly and singly pick every candidate, but when he does not make the selection himself, it is because he has ceded that power to regional strong men, governors, and other political associates who make the decisions for him. These politicians are constrained from nominating candidates against the wishes of the president by their own dependence on him. For example, the national president of the Central Executive

Committee of the PRI and the secretary-general of that committee are picked by the president. The president and executive committee of PRI at the regional level are picked by the state's municipal committees which in turn are chosen by the national Central Executive Committee of PRI.

Presidential control also operates in the party's three sectors—the agrarian, labor, and popular sectors. Those sectors are organized locally, regionally, and nationally like the PRI. Among other things, they may be involved in the formal and informal process of selecting candidates. Representatives of the three sectors are formally members of the national, state, and municipal nominating assemblies. Informally, they may be the regional strong men with whom the president consults. Not unlike other officials and politicians, however, they cannot get to these positions without having formerly received the approval of the president. In addition, their continued hold on these positions and other rewards depends on their relationship to the president.

In other words, obligations and loyalties throughout the political system flow upward (Hansen 1971:113) and follow the pattern known as patron-client relations in which patrons grant favors in return for political support, material goods, and/or other services (Hall 1977:510). This upward flow is in large part due to the president's power in the allocation of posts. The current president also picks his successor. In addition, the president appoints the twenty-one judges of the Supreme Court and through them the circuit and district court judges. The president can remove governors and through them he can remove municipal officers in thirteen states. The agrarian sector is dependent on the federal government for the granting of land. The labor sector is dependent on the federal government's right to declare strikes legal or illegal, to recognize a union or not, and to award other political posts. Finally, when all else fails, the president can use force.[1]

Given the high degree of formal and informal power in the hands of the Mexican president and a constitution which can accommodate either capitalism or socialism, the emphasis applied in economic development depends on who runs the government (Taylor 1960:731). There are a few observers of the Mexican political system who claim that the government is run by the masses through their participation in the party.[2] Most find it difficult to believe that a government run by the masses would continually sponsor legislation favoring the minority of agricultural and industrial elite.[3] To support their claim that it is a businessman's government, they cite the recipients of the benefits of national policies. As indicated in Chapter 1, government tax and expenditure policies have favored the industrial and commercial agricultural elite.

Consolidating this power even further, government expenditure is also primarily in the hands of the federal government. Municipios and states receive only a small proportion of tax revenues (see Table 13). That such a high proportion of the public treasury goes to the federal government has not only meant that the municipalities and states are dependent upon the federal government for appropriations—an important mechanism for maintaining the prevailing distribution of power—but also that the federal government, and only the federal government, could determine the course of growth, stagnation, or decline in particular localities.

Politics in San Cosme

The skewed distribution of economic and political power in Mexico has important consequences for a municipio such as San

Table 13
Public Treasury Allotments, 1958–1962
(in percentages)

YEAR	FEDERAL	STATES	FEDERAL DISTRICT	MUNICIPALITIES
1958	82	9	6	3
1959	77	10	10	3
1960	78	9	11	3
1961	77	9	12	3
1962	76	10	11	3

Source: *Anuario Estadistico de los Estados Unidos Mexicanos.* Cited in Casanova (1970:203).

Cosme.[4] First, it means that the decisions regarding all local political posts, including municipal offices and party and party sector committees, are made at the state level. Municipal candidates are selected at the state level and officials can be impeached by the state legislature. Similarly, the incumbents of posts of the party and its sectors are selected by the state organization. Second, the powers of a municipio are limited and many of its decisions are subject to approval by the state. Municipal budgets are small and must be approved by the state legislature. Any modifications of the approved budget must also be approved by the state legislature (*Periodico Oficial*, December 29, 1971:32). Largely for legal and financial reasons, the municipio cannot make its own public decisions. With their meager resources and powers, primary services, such as electricity and education, cannot be financed by municipios and therefore must be solicited from state and federal agencies.

The approved budget for San Cosme for 1972 allowed for expenses of 822 pesos for the year (see Figure 1). This was only 15 percent of what the municipio had collected the previous year. In 1971 a total of 5478 pesos was collected by San Cosme from taxes on the slaughter of cattle, licensing, new construction, the civil registry, tobacco, beer, matches, electricity, and property. This money goes to the state and cannot by spent by the community without the approval of the state legislature.

No one in San Cosme is a state or national politician. Consequently, decision-making in San Cosme is first of all an attempt to get access to the decision-makers outside the community. Without such access, government in the municipio is almost completely confined to administration, that is, the execution and organization of decisions made outside the community. With such access, decisions are still made outside the community but community members may be able to influence the outside decisions.

Factory work has given the obreros of San Cosme some access to outside power and money. Involvement in labor unions which are aligned with PRI enables workers to participate in the network of patron-client relations that extends throughout the Mexican political system.

Figure 1. Annual Budget for San Cosme for 1972 Fiscal Year (in pesos)

```
1.    Salary of Municipal President................120

2.    Salary of Municipal Secretary...............120

3.    Salary of Municipal Treasurer...............100

4.    Salary of Municipal Sub-Agent............... 96

5.    Salary of Municipal Judge................... 96

6.    Salary of Municipal Police Commander........ 50

7.    Office expenses for presidency.............. 60

8.    Office expenses for treasury................ 60

9.    Public works................................120
```

Patron-client relations, or clientelism, is a form of politics in which ties between leaders and followers are personal. The patron, a higher status person, uses his influence and resources to provide protection and/or benefits for a lower status person, the client, who in return gives general support and assistance (Scott 1977: 125). In the Mexican political system, such a system of political loyalties in return for personal positions and other rewards permeates the Mexican hierarchy.[5]

In San Cosme patron-client relations exist between local leaders and fellow San Cosmeros and between local leaders and regional and national leaders. As is true of most patrons, those in this study have many clients and are clients themselves to higher level patrons, that is, the patron-client networks are pyramided. Within the community, leaders or patrons offer jobs, bureaucratic knowledge, and political influence in return for political support and, to a lesser extent, financial contributions. Regional and national patrons similarly offer jobs, bureaucratic knowledge, and political support and occasional financial contributions.

Local Leaders and Their Clients

Most of San Cosme's patrons are or have been union leaders. Using their position, they control jobs in factories and because their factory unions are federated within the labor sector of PRI, they also control access to higher level labor and party leaders.[6] The local patrons use their control of jobs to get political support for themselves in local politics and to gather political support for their patrons outside San Cosme. While the greatest number of clients that a union leader has ever gotten by controlling jobs is only 125 men, the union leaders also use their union positions and worker support to tap into derived (state) power—that is, to get municipal posts which give them access to additional resources such as regular meetings with state officials, allocation of some municipal and other jobs, and some decision-making in the municipality.[7] With this additional power, they gain other clients.

The following case illustrates the use of both control of factory jobs and political resources by some of San Cosme's patrons. In 1967 the municipal authorities and the majority of those present at a municipal meeting voted to build a new school on the land of Juan Diaz.[8] Initially Diaz agreed to the purchase price of ten thousand pesos. Shortly thereafter, he decided he did not want to sell his land at that price. Diaz was a relatively well-off peasant with fifteen hectares who, until that time, had not been involved in community politics. He had neither patrons nor clients, not did he have political contacts who might help him fight the sale of his land. By aligning himself with several local patrons—two union leaders and a teacher—he managed to fight the sale for several years. Although he eventually lost, his patrons helped him by getting the new municipal president (whom they had put in office) to delay the building of the school.[9] When the opposition brought the issue to the state courts, his local patrons, using their state federation and party contacts, helped him to secure a lawyer, gave advice as to bureaucratic procedures, and informally spoke to state officials. He in return provided financial resources for them in this and other political conflicts in which they were engaged, and he and his family supported them in local politics.

Political support through the control of jobs was also important in this case. The dispute over Diaz's land eventually developed into a dispute over locating the new school in the second barrio (on Diaz's land) or in the fourth barrio. Several of the local leaders who lived in the fourth barrio wanted the school located there. The issue eventually divided most of the community; but whereas the leaders' choice of location was influenced by the barrio in which they lived, the nonleaders of the community made their choice, not according to where they lived, but where their union leaders lived. Many workers who lived in the second barrio supported locating the school in the fourth because their union leader was in favor in that location. Similarly, nonfactory workers who were clients of union leaders for political reasons supported the location of the school according to where the patron lived.[10] When the state court finally decided the issue in favor of locating the school in the second barrio, the leaders favoring the location of the fourth barrio proceeded to build their own school. In some cases a factory worker living close to his neighborhood school must send his children to a more distant school because his union leader (his patron) is supporting that school. Those people—mostly peasants—who are not clients of any leaders send their children to the nearest school.

Local Leaders as Clients

The position of the local union leaders is strongly influenced by the decisions of federation officials who are in turn under the PRI and business interests. In 1972 when a new factory was being opened in Tlaxcala, officials of the Confederación de Trabajadores de Mexico (CTM), one of the two main labor federations in Tlaxcala, told a San Cosme leader to collect names of men who wanted to work in the new factory. Local leaders also get more individualized job favors. For example, a retired union leader contacted his former federation leaders for help in obtaining a job for his daughter in a government office in Mexico City.

Most often, however, the local patrons exchange political support in return for help in community politics. Candidates for municipal positions are picked by state leaders for the state agrarian, popular, and labor sectors of the party. For a San Cosmero to be selected as a candidate for a municipal post, he needs someone to speak for him at the state level.[11] Similarly, since 1943 the state patrons have helped their San Cosme clients to get municipal status, electricity, potable water, a kindergarten, two new primary schools, a tele-secondary school, and drainage. The state patrons advise their clients where to go to request community development, speak to other state and national leaders on behalf of the San Cosmeros, and sometimes help with financial aid which they collect from clients elsewhere. The interaction of financial and political support was apparent in the request made by a state leader that the people of San Cosme make financial contributions (by buying raffle tickets) to the fire department of the city of Tlaxcala. He urged them to buy many tickets so that the next time he went to the governor on behalf of San Cosme he could remind the governor how generous the San Cosmeros had been.

OBREROS, THEIR WIVES, AND PEASANTS

As Bartra argues, there are two different political structures in Mexico: 1) The direct power structure of the bourgeoisie, and 2) a structure of mediation (1975:142). The direct power structure shows itself in the economic power of the agrarian and industrial bourgeoisie.[12] The "structure of mediation" is made up of such organizations as the CTM, and the labor and agrarian sectors of PRI. Although the structure of direct power is the real determinant of who has gained and who has lost from Mexican economic development, through the structure of mediation some of the demands of the poorer segments, such as the San Cosmeros, are satisfied.

The world of the factory workers includes some minimal access to the structure of mediation and through it to the economic and political resources that are concentrated at the top of the social pyramid. Involvement in labor unions, which are aligned with the PRI, has enabled them to meet and know state and national politicians to whom they can appeal for support, that is, with whom they can play the patron-client game. Rarely do peasants or proletarian women have this opportunity. There is an agrarian league in San Cosme but it is part of the labor sector and its leaders are former factory workers. If a peasant wants to make a demand, he or she must first go to a factory worker. The factory worker, on the other hand, goes to another factory worker or directly to a state leader. Peasants are rarely involved in politics except as followers or at the instigation of a non-peasant; a peasant woman who successfully solicited a milk program was asked by a teacher to go to the governor to make the request for the milk program because she, a peasant, was more humble in appearance. Another indication of the limited political participation of campesinos is that a peasant has never been municipal president.

Similarly, since community politics depends on supracommunity contacts and control of jobs or other resources to which most women do not have access, community decisions are made primarily by men. There was a woman municipal president in the 1970s, a retired schoolteacher who had been a widow for twenty-five years. Through her involvement in the school system she had developed ties to various state leaders, including several governors. She was selected as the candidate by the state party at a time when community factionalism was at its peak and the party was looking for a relatively neutral candidate. Although she had always been influential in the community because she is an unusually well informed, intelligent, and hard working person and relatively wealthy, she does not have a following because she does not control factory jobs. While she was in office she had derived state power. When she is out of office, she gets most of her support indirectly by aligning herself with union leaders or municipal officials. By 1980 there was a local Agrupación Nacional Feminina Revolucionaria (ANFER), a women's group that is part of PRI. Their political participation was confined to such activities as showing up in the state capital to support the PRI candidate for governor. In return they got bus fare and lunch.

Peasants and proletarian women have benefitted to some extent from the efforts of the obreros. Municipal status, potable water, improved education, drainage, and so forth are community services to which all San Cosmeros have access. But, not only are the decisions as to what demands to press for made by the proletarian men (within the limits of what the State is willing to consider), income also influences one's ability to take advantage of these services. Proletarian women often enjoy these benefits only through their dependence on their husbands. Peasants may not enjoy them at all because often they cannot afford the extra costs involved in taking advantage of public services which require the expenditure of some money, for example, for books for school children or a shower to make use of the community drainage system.

The obreros are by no means the privileged group that some observers have suggested. As indicated earlier, the salaries of the factory workers are low. According to the 1970 census, 80 percent of the industrial workers earned 1000 pesos a month or less (US $80.00). At least 30 percent earned less than the minimum wage (see Table 14). In 1980, a relatively well paid obrero, who had worked in factories for thirty-five years, was earning 6200 pesos (US $275.55) a month. Out of this he had to pay 90 pesos a month for rent, 1700 pesos a month for meals, and 350 pesos a month for transportation to and from Mexico City. After giving his wife 2000 pesos for household expenses he was left with 1900 pesos for his clothes, daily carfare, recreation, taxes, union dues and other expenses. The remainder, though limited, could be saved towards

Table 14
Monthly Income of San Cosmeros in 1969

PESOS PER MONTH	FACTORY WORKERS IN SAN COSME		PEASANTS IN SAN COSME	
	%	No.	%	No.
Not declaring	1.7	5	10.3	77
0 to 199	9.0	26	37.5	281
200 to 499	20.8	60	49.6	372
500 to 999	49.5	143	1.6	12
1,000 to 1,499	16.6	48	.3	2
1,500 to 2,499	2.1	6	.3	2
Over 2,500	.4	1	.5	4

Source: Dirección General de Estadísticas, 1970.

a television, a store, land, a gas stove, or other large items. Usually he consulted his wife but the ultimate decision rested with him and sometimes he made the decision alone. In this case the wife supplemented the husband's earnings by selling small quantities of corn and sewing for sale. Most of her earnings, however (under 1000 pesos a month), were used for necessary household expenses. She could not pay school tuition on a regular basis, or decide to buy a television.

The income of peasants allows them even less participation in the modern economy. Although they are taxed in cash or labor to help pay for such community improvements as electricity or schools, often they cannot afford to take advantage of the improvements. According to the 1970 census, 97 percent of the peasants reported earning less than 500 pesos a month and 42 percent had incomes of less than 200 pesos a month. By 1980 peasants were supplementing their income from agriculture with as much wage work as they could find. But the wages they received were significantly less and the work was more sporadic. A relatively well paid peasant earned only 150 pesos a day as a mason. For field work other then plowing, peasants earn 60 pesos a day. Plowing, which includes providing the plow and animals, pays 200 pesos a day, but increasingly tractors owned by non-peasants and often by non-San Cosmeros are being hired, and the demand for peasant labor in this more lucrative area is declining.

The greater earnings of factory workers enable them to live more comfortably. As indicated in Table 15, obreros are more likely to live in cement houses, whereas peasants live in adobe houses. More than three-fourths of the obreros had televisions by 1979, compared to only 32 percent of the campesinos. Obreros are also more likely to have gas stoves and sleep on beds rather than petates. Observations of and discussions with factory workers and their families suggest that they also drink milk and eat meat and eggs more frequently. Peasants do so rarely. For example, one peasant woman said they eat meat once a week and then it is usually a soup made mostly with bones. Another peasant family eats meat only on fiestas. Neither family drank milk on a regular basis. The wife of an obrero, however, said she cooks meat three or four times a week and has milk delivered daily.

Table 15
Living Conditions of Peasants and Factory Workers
in San Cosme

	PEASANT HOUSEHOLDS		PROLETARIAN HOUSEHOLDS	
	No.	%	No.	%
Cement house	11	10.0	36	42.4
Adobe house	98	89.9	49	57.6
Bed	57	51.8	78	91.8
Petate	53	48.2	7	8.2
Gas Stove	17	15.7	39	45.9
Wood	91	84.3	46	54.1
Television and Radio	34	32.1	65	76.5
Radio only	68	64.2	17	20.0
Neither	4	3.8	3	3.5

Source: Author's census of Section One, 1980.

Even the free public services of the community cannot be taken advantage of by peasants to the same extent as by factory workers. Making use of the drainage system that was being installed in 1980 requires, for example, an investment of several thousand pesos for a shower or toilet. Enrolling children in school entails the loss of the labor of children as well as fees for registration, uniforms, school supplies, costumes for school performances, and donations for various school events. That proletarian males utilize and derive the greatest advantage from community improvements is apparent in Table 16. Proletarian children are more likely than peasant children to have completed secondary school (the highest level of education available in San Cosme), and proletarian males are the most likely to have done so.

The gap between factory workers and peasants is apparent if one compares the lifestyle of a factory worker to that of a peasant. Don

Table 16
Education of Fifteen- to Nineteen-Year-Olds in San Cosme

| | PEASANTS | | | | FACTORY WORKERS | | | |
| | Sons | | Daughters | | Sons | | Daughters | |
	No.	%	No.	%	No.	%	No.	%
Less than nine years of school	16	80	19	90.5	14	46.7	33	89.2
Completed secondary school or more	4	20	2	9.5	16	53.3	4	10.8
Total	20	100	21	100.0	30	100.0	37	100.0

Source: Author's census, 1980.

Julio is a fifty-year-old factory worker who has worked in textile factories in Mexico City and Puebla for thirty years. He and his family live in a predominantly plastered-over adobe house which includes a large room with a table and chairs at which guests are served, a bed for Julio and Doña Maria, his wife, a sewing machine, a bureau, and a television; a smaller bedroom with two beds for their three unmarried sons; a traditional kitchen of adobe with a stone hearth where tortillas are made; and a second kitchen built of cement blocks which has a table at which the family eats, a gas stove, and a cupboard for pots and dishes. Julio and Maria have four children. The eldest, a son of twenty-six, dropped out of high school after one year. He is an obrero who also studies music and plays in a rock group. The next child, a twenty-five-year old daughter, is a nurse who lives in Mexico City with her husband, an obrero, and their three-month old child. A sixteen-year-old son is in his second year of high school in Puebla and the youngest child, a boy of seven, is in elementary school. Julio is active in local politics and has made numerous trips to Mexico City and Tlaxcala to get additional educational facilities for the community. Maria has swept classrooms, sold food at school fundraising events, and cooked for officials who have visited their home. Until about five years ago, the field work on the couple's three hectares (most of which was purchased after Julio became a factory worker) was done by Julio, the two oldest sons, and hired workers. Maria and the daughter stayed at home and prepared a meal for Julio, the two sons, and the hired workers when they returned. Now, Julio and his sons rarely go to the fields and they rely almost exclusively on hired field labor.

The family goes to Puebla often to shop and occasionally, for example, during Easter, they go to the movies. They frequently have visitors from other communities. In addition to the visiting officials mentioned above, Maria is from another community and her sisters and brothers often come to visit. Co-workers of Julio also visit them and at least a few times a year they return these visits.

Don Pedro is a forty-seven-year old campesino. Except for six months twenty years ago when he worked in the United States, he has always been a campesino and a part-time musician. He, his wife Doña Celia, and their three unmarried children live in a plastered-over adobe house which includes one room with two beds, a table and chairs, and baskets in which clothes are stored; and a traditional adobe kitchen with a stone hearth and some low chairs on which the family sits when they eat. Pots and dishes are hung from the walls or on a shelf. The couple's oldest child, a twenty-two-year old daughter, is a homemaker with six years of schooling. She and her husband, a factory worker, live with their three children, ranging in age from one to seven, and her husband's parents in San Cosme. Pedro and Celia also have a twenty-year-old son, also with six years of school, who is a factory worker in Puebla, a thirteen-year-old daughter who is in the seventh grade in San Cosme, and a seven-year-old son who is in elementary school. Pedro does most of the agricultural work on their lands (also three hectares but all of it is inherited), and he takes care of the family's pigs and oxen. Maria does some of the agricultural work; she usually goes with Pedro to the mountain for wood and she works in the fields during planting and harvesting. Pedro is not active in local politics. Although he sometimes plays music in neighboring communities, he and his family rarely visit outside of San Cosme and they rarely have outsiders visit them. Most of their shopping is also done in San Cosme.

Factory work has not only changed the nature of work and the conditions under which the obreros labor, but it has also increased their standard of living and given them some access to decision makers outside the community. With their extra income they can participate in a number of modern developments including the use of such modern consumer goods as televisions, beds, gas stoves, and modern medicine. They are even able to invest some of their extra income in such relatively lucrative economic activities as a store, a taxi, or a truck. Peasants and proletarian women have fewer economic resources at their disposal, are even more peripheral to the political system, and are participating to a lesser extent in the gains such as education. The world of obreros is one of active participation in industrial capitalism, not only as workers but as consumers and as party followers as well. Their wives, however, are not only excluded from working in the capitalist sector and driven out of subsistence production by competition with the capitalist sector, but are also excluded from the other activities of their husbands, such as decision-making both for the community and for the family. Peasants too are excluded from the work, the politics, and the consumption in which obreros participate.

OBREROS AND THE CLASS STRUCTURE

Neither exclusion nor inclusion, however, means immunity from the contradictions inherent in dependent industrial capitalism. Looked at over time and in the larger context of capitalist industrialization, the gains of the obreros are very tenuous.

First, as indicated in Chapter 1, the benefits they have derived over the last forty years occurred at a time when industrial productivity soared. The value of the output of the textile industry (that is, their sector) increased in just ten years from 11.5 million pesos in 1965 to 27.8 million in 1975, or almost two and a half times (calculated from Juarez 1979:137). But the rapid pace of economic development that characterized the first thirty-five years of the Mexican "miracle" is not continuing. After growth rates of 8.8 percent between 1960 and 1965 (Gollás and García Rocha 1976:424), manufacturing production increased by only 4.1 percent in 1975, 2.8 percent in 1976, and 3.0 percent in 1977 (Economic Commission for Latin America 1978:329).

Whether the obreros will retain their gains and continue to benefit is not dependent merely on the overall dynamism of the economy. Peasants and proletarian women failed to benefit from even very dynamic growth. Other changes associated with industrial capitalism, aside from a slowing down of growth, suggest also that for workers such as those of San Cosme the gains are ephemeral.

The Mexican economy is becoming increasingly dominated by monopoly rather than competitive capitalism. One estimate for the overall concentration index of Mexican industry is 43 percent. That is, the four largest enterprises account for 43 percent of all industrial production (Baird and McCaughan 1979:90). As capital becomes increasingly concentrated, both in industry and agriculture, unemployment has risen and the labor force has been reorganized. In the textile industry, for example, during the same period mentioned above when the value of production more than doubled, the number of establishments declined by 12 percent and the number of textile workers declined by 16.5 percent (calculated from Juarez 1979:138). As monopolistic capital-intensive firms (many of them foreign-owned), come to dominate the economy, unemployment rises and the large labor reserve keeps wages down. According to the most recent United Nations report, real wages have decreased (Economic Commission for Latin America 1978: 336). High unemployment and low wages attract still more foreign and concentrated capital.[13]

For semiskilled textile workers such as those of San Cosme, the backdrop of high and increasing unemployment is further aggravated by the increasing stratification of the work force and the downgrading of their jobs.

As Braverman (1974) and others, following Marx, have shown, technological changes under industrial capitalism not only reduce the number of workers needed but also redivide labor so that instead of a unified and homogeneous working class, the labor process and the labor markets are segmented (Edwards, Gordon and Reich 1971:201). In this segmenting or Balkanizing of the labor force the operations involved in the production process are broken down and assigned to different workers requiring different degrees of knowledge and/or training. The worker loses control over the labor process, that is, becomes alienated, and labor power is cheapened. By separating conception and execution, less skilled, lower paid, and interchangeable workers can perform routinized and standardized segments of production. As Braverman suggests:

> Every step in the labor process is divorced, so far as possible, from specialized knowledge and training and reduced to simply labor. Meanwhile, the relatively few persons for whom specialized knowledge and training are reserved are freed so far as possible from the obligations of simple labor. In this way, a structure is given to all labor processes that at its extremes polarizes those whose time is infinitely valuable and those whose time is worth almost nothing. (1974:82–83)

For the obreros of San Cosme deskilling has come about with the introduction of new, usually imported, more advanced and more productive textile machinery. The obrero now watches more machines and when they break down he is unable to fix them. Instead of fixing them himself as he did formerly after he had some experience, he must wait for a mechanic or an engineer. His job has become more simplified and repetitive and he has become more easily replaceable.

The obreros are aware of deskilling, high unemployment, rapid turnover, and failure of wages to keep up with inflation. Their awareness of these processes is apparent in frequent discussion of inflation and the unavailability of jobs and their complaints and criticisms of the transnationals and *charro* (co-opted) leaders of the unions. Most of all their awareness is apparent in their hopes and efforts for their children. It is here too, however, that the basic nature of capitalism, inequality, and the even greater inequalities inherent in dependent capitalism will exclude them from the gains of increased production as it has excluded women and peasants.

NOTES

1. For a discussion of the use of force see Stevens (1974).

2. See Needler (1971) and Scott (1969).

3. See Brandenburg (1964), Hansen (1971) and K. Johnson (1971).

4. This and the next two sections are slightly revised from Rothstein (1979).

5. For discussions of patron-client relations at other levels in the Mexican system see Fagen and Tuohy (1972), Miller (1973), Cornelius (1977), Eckstein (1977), and Grindle (1977).

6. While not all factory unions in Mexico are so federated, the unions that are important in San Cosme politics, and to most San Cosmeros who work in factories, are members of the state federations and the national confederations, either the Confederation of Mexican Workers (CTM) or the Revolutionary Confederation of Mexican Workers (CROM).

7. See Stuart (1972:36) for a discussion of derived state power.

8. All personal names have been changed.

9. Because of the Mexican law against re-election, leaders can only hold the presidency for one term of three years. They often, therefore, put clients in political posts and control municipal politics indirectly.

10. Nonfactory workers indebted to leaders include those whom union leaders have helped to obtain political posts, commercial licenses, or other benefits.

11. Being selected as the PRI candidate is tantamount to winning the election as the PRI candidates have always won.

12. For a related discussion of the two structures of power in advanced capitalist states see Miliband (1969).

13. A United States Department of Commerce pamphlet entitled "Investing in Mexico" points out that unemployment is high, wages are low, and minimum wage laws are not always enforced (Bastian 1979:6).

6

The World of Children

Capitalist industrialization has had as one of its major consequences in San Cosme the creation of two different worlds for women and men. By changing the unit and locus of production from the family and the family farm to the factory and by restricting the employment of women, capitalist industrialization has narrowed and privatized the sphere of proletarian women. This private world is centered physically and socially on the home and the family. Consumption, rather than production, is its focus. The new world of men presents a sharp contrast to the private world of women. The men's world is physically and socially removed from the home and the family. The life of the men, the primary and often exclusive wage earners, is centered in the public sphere. They work in a public world and even when they are in the community, they are often to be found in such public places as stores and municipal offices where they meet to socialize and politic.

Along with the separation of the family and the family economy into these two worlds, a third world of children and childhood has been created by proletarianization.

THE MALLEABILITY OF THE LIFE CYCLE

Since the seminal work by Ariès in 1962, *Centuries of Child-hood*, social scientists have come to recognize what Katz and Davey call "the malleability of the life cycle" (1978:S82). In this view the stages of life, including childhood, are seen to be variable.

According to Ariès, in the Middle Ages childhood was brief. At about the age of seven, children entered "the great community of men, sharing in the work and play of their companions, old and young alike" (1962:411). Then, at the beginning of modern times, with the revival of education, a new attitude toward children emerged. "It was recognized that the child was not ready for life, and that he had to be subjected to a special treatment, a sort of quarantine, before he was allowed to join adults" (Ariès 1962:412). This new childhood was characterized by a separation of children from adults, the prolongation of childhood, the centering of the family on children, and an increasing concern with education.

It is this new attitude toward children and childhood, hereafter referred to as child-centeredness, that now characterizes the proletarians of San Cosme. This is apparent in four changes in childhood in San Cosme: 1) Children are less integrated into the adult world; 2) instead they are "quarantined" in their own world of school; 3) proletarian children are integrated into the adult world later than they are in the peasant economy; and 4) parents are devoting more time, energy, and resources to their children in order to educate them.

CHILD-CENTEREDNESS IN SAN COSME

The labor of children is as important a part of the peasant family economy in San Cosme as it was in the Middle Ages, according to Ariès. Increasingly, however, children are being separated from the adult world and placed in a world of school and other children. This is apparent in the level of education now achieved. As Table 17 indicates, among those fifty years of age and older, 97 percent *did not* complete primary school. Among the fifteen- to nineteen-year-olds, however, 94 percent *did* complete primary school (see Figure 2 for an outline of the educational system of Tlaxcala).

A Separate World

School attendance means that children are away from home and farm and thus unavailable for at least five hours a day. Traveling may keep them away from San Cosme an additional two hours a day. Some children live elsewhere so they can attend a particular school. Homework and studying for entrance examinations also keep children away from the work and play of adults.

Table 17
Years of Schooling of San Cosmeros

AGE	LESS THAN 6 YEARS		6 YEARS		MORE THAN 6 YEARS		TOTAL	
	No.	%	No.	%	No.	%	No.	%
50 and over	104	97.2	3	2.8	0	—	107	100.0
40–49	84	87.5	12	12.5	0	—	96	100.0
30–39	68	80.0	15	17.6	2	2.4	85	100.0
20–29	19	41.3	26	56.5	1	2.2	46	100.0
15–19	8	6.0	85	63.4	41	30.6	134	100.0

Source: Author's census, 1980.
Note: See Figure 2 for an outline of the educational system of Tlaxcala.

Presumably, since they are not in school all day and every day, children could help in the fields or in the home during their free hours. Many of the children do. The children of factory workers, however, are less likely to do so. The author's census in 1980 included a series of questions on the ages children began performing various tasks. Among campesinos only 38 percent of the children seven and over had not yet begun to help in the harvest. Among obreros 64 percent of those seven and over had not yet begun to help in the harvest. Even during the summer vacation, when most of the spot observations were done, proletarian children were less likely to help with agricultural tasks. Among campesinos there was only one family out of eight in which children did not do any agricultural work during the study period of the spot observations. Among the fifteen proletarian families, children did not do any agricultural work in five families.

In part the withdrawal of proletarian children from agricultural work is due to the general lessening of subsistence cultivation for all proletarian family members. As indicated in Chapter 5, although proletarian families still cultivate some corn, because of the unpro-

Figure 2. Educational System of Tlaxcala

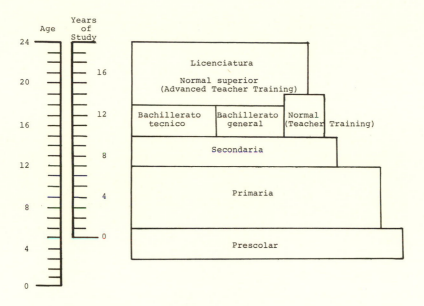

Source: Dirección General de Planeacion (1975).

ductivity of small-scale agriculture, they are less likely to plant squash and beans as well, and they weed and check their fields less. They are more likely than peasants to hire workers to replace men, women, and children of the family. That the lesser involvement of proletarian children in agriculture is not entirely due to more hired labor and fewer agricultural tasks, however, is suggested by the fact that proletarian children are also less likely to do household chores. In eight of the fifteen proletarian families, that is, 60 percent, children did no housework during the observations. There was only one peasant family in which children did no housework.

These findings are true regardless of sex. None of the studies of child-centeredness systematically compare sons and daughters. Ariès, however, suggests that "The idea of childhood profited the

Table 18
Type of Work Done By Children in San Cosme

| | PROLETARIAN FAMILIES | | | | PEASANT FAMILIES | | | |
| | Sons | | Daughters | | Sons | | Daughters | |
	No.	%	No.	%	No.	%	No.	%
Agricultural Work								
Yes	8	66.7	4	30.8	6	85.7	2	28.6
No	4	33.3	9	69.2	1	14.3	5	71.4
Total	12	100.0	13	100.0	7	100.0	7	100.0
Domestic Work								
Yes	2	16.7	7	53.8	1	14.3	6	85.7
No	10	83.3	6	46.2	6	85.7	1	14.3
Total	12	100.0	13	100.0	7	100.0	7	100.0

Source: Spot observations of eight peasant and fifteen proletarian families.

boys first of all while the girls persisted much longer in the traditional way of life which confused them with adults" (1962:61).

As Table 18 indicates, proletarian daughters do less domestic
work than do peasant daughters. Similarly, proletarian sons do less
agricultural work than do peasant sons.

At least through the sixth grade proletarian daughters are
quarantined like their brothers (see Table 19). The differential
benefits of which Ariès speaks appear later. Although the
educational level of peasant children is lower, most peasant
children (almost 80 percent) are now also separated from the adult
world while they are in elementary school for six years.

A More Prolonged Childhood

Childhood is not only increasingly separate from the adult world
but children in San Cosme are also entering the adult world later
and in a less graduated fashion.

Table 19
Years of Schooling of Twelve- to Nineteen-Year-Olds
in San Cosme

| | PEASANTS | | | | FACTORY WORKERS | | | |
| | Sons | | Daughters | | Sons | | Daughters | |
	No.	%	No.	%	No.	%	No.	%
Less than 6 years	8	21.1	7	21.9	4	7.2	3	5.7
6 or more years	30	78.9	25	78.1	51	92.7	50	94.3
Total	38	100.0	32	100.0	55	99.9	53	100.0

Source: Author's census, 1980.

In the family economy children begin such productive and domestic tasks as caring for animals, sweeping, and running errands by the age of six or seven. Gradually they assume more responsible jobs. At about the age of eight they may cut weeds and make tortillas. By ten or twelve they can plant, harvest, and make meals. Temporary patrilocal residence (that is, living with the groom's parents during the early years of marriage) and the practice of giving a newly married couple only part of the land that they would eventually inherit meant also that even after marriage the transition to independence in consumption and production was gradual. But by the age of thirteen children had already begun doing the tasks that would be their life's work.

Today, however, many children are still in school at the age of thirteen. Almost a third of the fifteen- to nineteen-year-olds have gone beyond the sixth grade. They may occasionally participate in adult activities but often they cannot. Some families try to do their harvesting on the weekends so that children in school can help. Many, however, just do without the labor of their children. There is no high school in San Cosme so after the ninth grade (secondary school), students must spend time traveling to other communities. Since the local secondary school is a tele-secondary school, and some families prefer to send their children to a secondary school where teaching is direct, a number of children go elsewhere even before high school. Frequently they live where they study and return home only on weekends. Since post-primary school is most likely to take children out of San Cosme, this is the time when they are least likely to be involved in the adult world.

The prolongation of childhood is most apparent among proletarian sons for whom some post-primary school has become the norm. More of the sons of factory workers between fifteen and nineteen have gone beyond primary school than not (see Table 20). It is during adolescence that proletarian sons get tracked for the adult world of males and proletarian daughters get tracked for the adult world of females. Most of the daughters of the obreros have not gone beyond the sixth grade. Here too the differentiation between proletarian males and peasants is most apparent.

The girls who do not continue in school follow one of several paths. Most stay home and help their mothers. Or, as one proletarian woman described it, they do "nothing."[1] Some get married. A few go to work as domestics in Puebla or Mexico City.

Table 20
Post-Primary Education of Fifteen- to Nineteen-Year-Olds in San Cosme

	SIX YEARS OR FEWER		SEVEN OR MORE YEARS		TOTAL	
	No.	%	No.	%	No.	%
Peasant Daughters	17	81.0	4	19.0	21	100.0
Peasant Sons	16	80.0	4	20.0	20	100.0
Proletarian Daughters	28	75.6	9	24.3	37	99.9
Proletarian Sons	11	36.7	19	63.3	30	100.0

Source: Author's census, 1980.

Table 21
Principal Occupation of Teenage Girls in San Cosme

	NUMBER	PERCENTAGE
Student	23	41.8
Homemaker	28	50.9
Maid	2	3.6
Obrera	1	1.8
Teacher	1	1.8
Total	55	99.9

Source: Author's census, 1980.

Table 22
Age at Marriage for Women in San Cosme

	NUMBER
14 Years Old	4
15 Years Old	8
16 Years Old	18
17 Years Old	15
18 Years Old	17
19 Years Old	10
20 Years Old	7
21 – 24	17
25 – 29	10
30 – 39	7
40 and older	6
Total	119

Source: Municipal records of San Cosme for 1977, 1978, and 1979.

This is particularly true of those who come from poorer families and have not completed primary school. A still small but increasing number go to work on what Ehrenreich and Fuentes call the "global assembly line" (1981). That is, they work as unskilled or semi-skilled workers in transnational companies such as Exquisiteform in the city of Tlaxcala, or Majestic in Calpulalpan. Since these companies only employ young women, this represents only a temporary break before domesticity.

For the majority of teenaged girls childhood is terminated at about age thirteen (see Table 21). The next few years are spent practicing domestic skills and, to a lesser extent, agricultural skills. Most are married before they are nineteen. As indicated in Table 22, the modal age of women who got married in 1977, 1978, or 1979 was sixteen and more than half (52 percent) were married between the ages of fourteen and eighteen.[2]

Many of the teenaged boys continue in school through the ninth grade (about age fifteen). At that point they must make the abrupt transition to the men's world of wage work. It is made somewhat smoother, however, by the practice of serving an apprenticeship under a relative, and, as indicated in Chapter 5, they usually begin factory work nearby in Puebla. By this time they have usually been participating in the public sphere to a greater extent than their sisters. Even though they have been segregated in the world of school, children still help their parents to some extent. The girls, who as indicated earlier primarily do domestic tasks, tend to stay in or close to the house. The boys, who usually help in agricultural activities, go out to the fields or mountain. Their leisure hours are also more likely to be spent in public places whereas girls relax in their own home or at the home of a friend or relative (see Table 23).

With proletarianization, childhood has been prolonged and participation in the economic activities of adults is delayed. But, although children do not enter "the community of men" until later, preparation for the two different worlds of men and women begins early. Initially girls as well as boys are sent off to the world of children: school. During adolescence, however, proletarian boys continue to prepare longer for the men's public world. Whereas teenaged daughters of obreros enter the world of women at the ages of thirteen, fourteen, and fifteen, teenaged sons of factory workers stay in school. This educational gap between proletarian males and

Table 23
Leisure Time Locations of Sons and Daughters
in San Cosme

	IN THE HOUSE		IN THE STREET		TOTAL	
	No.	%	No.	%	No.	%
Proletarian Daughters	63	92.6	5	7.4	68	100.0
Proletarian Sons	39	46.4	45	53.6	84	100.0
Peasant Daughters	10	100.0	0	—	10	100.0
Peasant Sons	11	57.9	8	42.1	19	100.0

Source: Spot observations of eight peasant and fifteen proletarian families.

females will undoubtedly have repercussions on male-female relations within and outside the family.

The Costs of Child-Centeredness

As Minge-Kalman and others have suggested the delayed integration of children into the adult world has high costs in foregone labor—nor are these the only costs of prolonged childhood.[3] The parents of San Cosme, especially the proletarians, are paying more for childhood in other ways as well. Increasingly, a variety of efforts and resources are devoted by parents to their children.

To say that proletarians are increasingly devoted to children is not to say, as Shorter (1975) suggests, that peasants are indifferent to or neglect their children. It is only by ignoring the high costs involved that one can characterize peasants as indifferent or negligent. Peasants are poor; they not only lack excess resources to devote to children but are often living below a subsistence level. One peasant family, for example, had to cut out meat completely so that they could send their daughter to school. Factory workers, who earn at least 1200 pesos a week compared to a well-paid peasant's 720 pesos, can forego the labor of children and hire workers or buy some of the products, such as alfalfa instead of weeds to feed animals, that the labor of children might otherwise provide. Also, as the family economy becomes less productive, peasant families rely heavily on the wages that their sons can earn as factory workers and to a lesser extent on the wages of daughters working as domestics. One peasant woman said that she had wanted her fourteen-year-old daughter to continue in school but the family needed the money, so the daughter went to work as a maid in Mexico City. Obreros can also use their earnings to buy a television for a child who cries for a t.v., to buy school uniforms or a costume so that their child could dance or be king in a school performance, and to pay four or five hundred pesos a month (plus the cost of books, bus fare, registration fees, and clothes) for tuition for private school.

Obreros also have the political contacts to fight for improved educational facilities which are scarce in Mexico, especially in rural areas. Factory workers have made numerous trips to Tlaxcala and Mexico City to plead their case for more schools. They have helped construct and finance the schools. They also serve on school committees. Proletarian women sweep classrooms and cook and sew for school fiestas.

In sum, San Cosmeros now devote a great deal of their time, effort, and resources to childhood. Rather than being a gradual and increasing integration into the adult world, it has become a long and costly period of preparation away from but for the adult world of wage labor. Even the girls who will work only temporarily as obreras need a sixth grade certificate. This costly preparation has involved the efforts of individuals, families, and the community. It is important to stress that all members of the family are involved. There has been a tendency in much of the literature on child-centeredness to focus on mothers.[4] The data from San Cosme indicate that although the nature of their efforts differ—mothers cook and clean for the schools and must take over domestic chores children would do if they were not in school, fathers go to work in factories and go to see state and national politicians, and children try to get through an educational system that must, because educational facilities are very scarce, eliminate many—child-centeredness is a costly process for everyone.

CHILD-CENTEREDNESS, EDUCATION,
AND PROLETARIANIZATION

Ariès suggests that child-centeredness emerged in modern times with the revival of the concern for education (1962). He also notes a connection between the emergence of the middle class and the new attitude towards children. He does not, however, systematically examine the relationship of class, concern for education, and child-centeredness. As Minge-Kalman points out, Ariès asks, but does not answer, "How did we come from that ignorance of childhood to the centering of the family around the child in the nineteenth century?" (1978:457)

Several more recent studies have suggested that the emergence of the idea of childhood, the centering of the family on children, and the increasing concern for education that Ariès describes are related to the development of wage labor and proletarianization. More specifically, these studies suggest that as the Industrial Revolution progressed the demand for educated labor increased. An educated labor force is more skilled and is socialized to the discipline of the factory system, including concern with time and submission to authority. Initially the demand was only for some education. Gradually, because education serves a number of functions, more education was required. In addition to providing skills, knowledge, and socialization, education reduces unemployment by furnishing jobs for teachers, administrators, and others and by postponing the age of entry into the work force. Education is also a way of screening out job applicants when there are not enough jobs. Since, as Gintis suggests, one of the main outcomes of the school system is that the student learns to operate in an alienated educational environment which reproduces faithfully the capitalist work environment (1971:276), educational criteria for jobs may also screen out potential troublemakers. In conjunction with the segmentation of the labor force, as discussed earlier in Chapter 5, educational requirements also screen job applicants so as to increase the value of a small segment of the labor force while cheapening the value of the labor of the majority. Finally, as will be discussed in the concluding chapter, educational achievement also offers a rationale for the inequality inherent in capitalism.

Independence Day, 1971. Children were not required to wear uniforms. *Photograph by the author.*

Independence Day, 1980. Only children wearing uniforms could march. The building on the left is the tele-secondary school. *Photograph by the author.*

As both Ariès and Minge-Kalman note, it is education that extends and redefines childhood (Minge-Kalman 1978:461). In creating the new childhood the family too "underwent a qualitative change as a labor unit—from one that produced food to one whose primary function was to socialize and educate laborers for an industrial labor market" (Minge-Kalman 1978:462). As Tilly and Scott similarly point out, "Not property or skill or money but good training, discipline and opportunity were what parents gave children 'to start them out in life' " (1978:212). As the costs to the family increased, of school itself and also of the foregone labor, children "subtly but rapidly developed into a labor-intensive, capital-intensive product of the family in industrial society" (Minge-Kalman 1978:466).

The parallels between the nineteenth century European experience and the emergence of child-centeredness in San Cosme is a further verification of the relationship between industrialization, proletarianization, concern with education, and child-centeredness. Until recently the men from San Cosme were able to obtain first unskilled and then semiskilled jobs in textile factories by knowing someone in the factory and making a gift to the union leader. Today, however, job applicants even for unskilled jobs in these same factories must not only know someone but also have a sixth grade diploma. As Mexico becomes more industrialized, the government's concern for education has also increased. The budget for education has been increased and government sponsored signs and radio and television announcements urge parents to enroll their children in school. Although the government has expanded its support, the bulk of the costs of upgrading the labor force have fallen on the workers themselves. This is apparent in the fact that in the state of Tlaxcala, although school enrollment more than doubled between 1970 and 1974, more than half of the increment was due to the increased enrollment in private school (see Table 24). In addition to the costs of private school tuition, families pay transportation costs, registration fees, labor to replace their absent children, and other expenses.

Instead of asking why the attitude towards children has changed, perhaps Ariès' question should have been why do families take on these high costs and the burden of self-upgrading? In large part San

Table 24
School Enrollment in Tlaxcala

	FEDERAL	STATE	PRIVATE	TOTAL
1970–71	353	707	609	1,669
1971–72	670	709	638	2,018
1972–73	838	814	920	2,572
1973–74	1,043	850	1,518	3,411

Source: Dirección General de Planeacion Educative (1975).

Cosmeros bear this burden because they have no choice. Everyone in San Cosme is aware that their children cannot support themselves as peasants and that they will have to be wage laborers. They are also all aware that to be even a sweeper in a textile factory, a sixth grade education is necessary. But the concern of San Cosmeros (especially the proletarians) and the Mexican government goes beyond a sixth grade diploma. Many San Cosmeros do not want their children to be factory workers. One proletarian father, for example, when asked whether it was better to be a peasant or an obrero replied, "Neither. It is better to have a career." San Cosmeros see education as the means by which their children will achieve some social mobility.

The idea that through education one's children can experience mobility is a common theme in the literature on modernization. It is also heard frequently in the appeals of social workers, nurses, and other reformers. And there are numerous examples of such mobility through education. What is often overlooked, however, is that although education has become necessary, it is not sufficient. By its very nature a capitalist class structure limits the number of successes. In a dependent capitalist system, such as that of Mexico, mobility is further limited.

The proletarian men of San Cosme have been relatively fortunate. Their wives and children have also derived some benefits from their proletarianization. However, the prospects for the children of San Cosme are less promising.

NOTES

1. The domestic role of adult women is not yet described as "nothing." That it is considered nothing for a teenaged girl may reflect acceptance of the pattern discussed in Chapter 4 in which domestic tasks are becoming the exclusive responsibility of mothers. It may also reflect the attitude among some proletarian parents that teenaged girls should also stay in school. One proletarian man, for example, urged a teenaged girl to continue on in school beyond the ninth grade, which she had completed. He said that she did not need a career that required a university education, but she should have some training such as that for a teacher or nurse. The daughter of the woman who made the comment that the teenaged girls were doing nothing is a nurse.

2. The municipal records from which these data were collected do not indicate whether these are first marriages. Some women may therefore have married earlier than the table suggests.

3. See also Schildkrout (1981).

4. See Shorter (1975) and Minge-Kalman (1978).

CHAPTER

7

Conclusion:
All for the Children

San Cosmeros, like many proletarians elsewhere, are aware that there are better jobs than the ones they have and they want their sons, and to a lesser extent their daughters, to have those jobs.[1] They are also aware that the better jobs require more education. Toward that end they have devoted a great deal of their time, efforts, and resources. Numerous sacrifices have been made. For example, one storeowner said he closed his store because the constant interruptions of customers disturbed his grandchildren while they were studying. Many families sacrifice meat so that they can send their children to school. One man in his early fifties said that his brother often asks him why he continues to work so hard as a factory worker. He said it is because he wants his children to be well-educated so that they will not have to be factory workers. Among the young adults, those in their twenties and early thirties, many intend to have only two children so that they can afford to educate them. Most of the parents, however, already have four, five, or six children. Their childbearing was done when infant mortality was still very high and children were not a labor and capital intensive product of the family. A high fertility rate was necessary to compensate for the high infant mortality rate and children, rather than being the object of much of the family's resources, could, with their labor, increase the family's resources. Although some of the older children help their parents and siblings by contributing part of their wages to the costs of educating their siblings, the major burden of educating a large family falls on the parents.[2] As Sennett and Cobb suggest in their Boston study, parents bear this burden because the strains of one's own life become justified by the privileges work will create for one's children (1972:124).

THE MYTH OF MOBILITY

The hopes of the San Cosmeros mirror the models of mainstream theorists and reformers who maintain that education is an equalizer in modern society. Such theorists see education as equalizing the gap between nations as well as within nations and often underdevelopment is attributed to the lack of education. Hughes, for example, suggests that the poverty of nations is attributable to the lack of education and this lack of education keeps poor nations poor (1970).

This view of education is part of the mainstream picture of modern society and the modern world as open, mobile societies in which equality and opportunity abound. According to this view, public education reduces traditional inequalities (Moore 1963:107) and blurs the distinction between masses and elites (Kahl 1968:5). Differences that persist, despite this presumed equality, are seen as the inevitable inequality of individual differences in individual ability.

This view, which hides, justifies, and legitimates inequality, does not explain the increasing gap between rich and poor in Mexico. Nor does it explain why most of the men in San Cosme, despite their greater education (see Table 25), are still doing the same work and earning the same salaries, in the same factories, on the same temporary contracts, as the generation before them. The women too are still homemakers dependent on their husbands' insecure and low-paying jobs.

The original factory workers in San Cosme, that is, the first generation, experienced mobility with the shift from peasant to obrero. Sons of peasants may still move upwards as they too become factory workers. Most likely, however, the rate of absorption will slow down. As indicated in Chapter 5, the number of textile workers has been declining. In the late 1970s, manufacturing in general had its capacity to generate employment reduced by a 1.6 percent cut in the personnel employed (Economic Commission

Table 25
Average Education of San Cosmeros

AGE	MEAN NUMBER OF YEARS OF SCHOOLING	
	Men	Women
12–14	5.96	5.84
15–19	7.01	6.52
20–29	5.47	4.63
30–39	3.81	3.53
40–49	3.0	2.56
50–59	2.11	1.76

Source: Author's census, 1980.

for Latin America 1978:338). There is also a growing tendency to hire more educated workers. Since peasant sons tend to be less educated, they may not be able to enter the industrial sector as easily as the first generation obreros. Some sons and daughters of peasants and semiskilled factory workers have become middle class teachers, nurses, lawyers, and engineers. The son of one factory worker, who is still in high school but has some mechanical training, works in the same factory as his father and earns almost as much at sixteen as his fifty-year-old father who has been an obrero all his life. As indicated in Table 26, however, the sons of most factory workers still become semiskilled factory workers. They work in the same textile industry which is one of the lowest-paying industries in Mexico. Inflation has meant that their real wages are less than the wages of obreros ten years ago. Their jobs have become redefined but rather than taking advantage of their improved education, their jobs are simplified and they are more easily replaced. In addition, as many young obreros point out, since the price of land in San Cosme has risen, they cannot afford to buy land as their fathers did and they cannot supplement their wages and carry themselves through periods of unemployment with subsistence production. If factories are built in San Cosme as is now being proposed, the possibility of supplementing their wages with subsistence production will be even further reduced. Education has not improved their standard of living.

The daughters of San Cosme are also unlikely to have experienced any significant changes in lifestyle through their improved education. The daughters of campesinos may experience a rise in their standard of living by becoming the housewife of an obrero. The majority of proletarian daughters become proletarian homemakers like their mothers (see Table 26). Most likely, also, the subsistence production which could give their mothers at least a small amount of economic independence will continue to decline. The increasing gap in education between husbands and wives will further increase their dependence.

Of the few San Cosmeros who have benefitted from more education, most have become nurses or teachers. It should be noted that between 1950 and 1970 education and health gained more in labor force representation than any other subsector (Munoz 1975:53). Whether even a small proportion of San Cosmeros can continue to experience mobility via these fields depends on the continued demand for health and education personnel.

The success stories of San Cosme are qualitatively impressive. Unfortunately, however, despite their improved education, and the costly efforts of all, the majority of the youth will do the same semiskilled, or less skilled, factory work that men from San Cosme have been doing since the 1940s. That is, they will not experience any mobility. Their wives too will do the same domestic activities as their mothers except their jobs will probably be less diverse and confined even more to consumption. Unlike their mothers, however, for whom proletarian domesticity meant a higher standard of living than that of their peasant parents, most proletarian daughters will not experience mobility through marriage. If they try to get jobs in the capitalist sector, they will find that their gender and lack of education will confine them to the least stable and lowest-paying positions. Within the home too, their educational inferiority and lesser knowledge of the public world will probably also further reinforce the authority of their husbands.

Table 26
Social Mobility in San Cosme

| | FATHER'S OCCUPATION | | | |
| | Obrero | | Campesino | |
	No.	%	No.	%
Occupation of				
Son (16 and over)				
Obrero	32	62.7	59	80.8
Campesino	0	—	4	5.5
Student	18	35.3	4	5.5
White Collar	0	—	3	4.1
Miscellaneous	1	2.0	3	4.1
Total	51	100.0	73	100.0
Occupation of				
Daughter				
(16 and over)				
Homemaker	22	62.9	37	72.5
Obrera	1	2.8	4	7.8
Campesina	0	—	1	2.0
Student	7	20.0	5	9.8
White Collar	3	8.6	4	7.8
Maid	1	2.8	0	—
Miscellaneous	1	2.8	0	—
Total	35	99.9	51	99.9

Source: Author's census, 1980.

According to Wells, peasants are characterized by a sense of powerlessness and see the world as uncontrollable. Those with modern values, on the other hand:

believe not only that the world is knowable and controllable but that it is to an individual's advantage to plan his or her life and to attend to the future as well as to the present and

the past. To merely avoid trouble is no longer enough (as it
was in traditional society) for the modern individual; such a
person wants to advance. . . (1978:521)

Child-centeredness is an attempt by San Cosmeros to plan for the
future and to deal with the strains of the present. They have hopes,
largely through education, for advancement. They are striving for
success *in* the system. They have become conscious of the occupational and status distinctions which divide the working class and
which encourage individualism. They have come to accept the
ideology of individualism that prevails in capitalist society: "If you
have sufficient merit, you rise up through the structure of classes till
you reach the level of society your talents permit" (Sennett and
Cobb 1972:250). Like the workers in Boston studied by Sennett and
Cobb they attribute their own poverty to lack of education and
their own failure to have continued on in school. One young
woman, for example, blamed herself for having quit school before
she completed elementary school and thus having to be a maid.
Frequently, people explicitly or implicitly suggested that a child
was not going on to secondary or high school because she or he did
not have the ability to get in. Parents too were sometimes blamed
for having too many children or not trying hard enough to send
their children to school; but many San Cosmeros are also aware of
the broader processes to which they are subject.

They are aware of the increased productivity in their factories
and their own declining real wages. They talked more often in 1980
than in the early 1970s about charro leaders and transnationals.
Proletarian homemakers are also aware of the insecurity of their
husband's jobs and that salaries are not rising as fast as prices.
Although older San Cosmeros talk, largely with approval, about
all the changes the community has experienced in the last forty
years, younger San Cosmeros stress that the community is not
changing and the people of San Cosme are still poor. They are both
right. The community has changed but it is still poor.

As Barkin suggests, "Education is not a system that can function
outside the larger social context" (1971:955, translation mine).
Education has an impact when the economy is able to provide an
adequate number of jobs (Muñoz, 1975:151). Mexico is constrained
by both capitalism and dependence from doing so. Some new

higher level jobs have been created but there are not enough jobs and the ability of the modern sector to generate jobs is declining. The ability of the traditional peasant economy to provide even a low level of subsistence has also declined. Many of the new jobs that are accompanying industrialization are either located in the home country of the transnational or are not high level professional jobs but rather deskilled and simplified segments of the production process. An insufficient number of deskilled jobs means that there are many without jobs who can easily replace those with jobs. Jobs become less secure and more poorly paid.

The obreros of San Cosme have never liked their jobs, but they and their families derived some advantages from them and had hopes that their children would be upwardly mobile. Whether they will continue to strive for success in the system if they no longer have even the hopes of such success seems unlikely. They may resign themselves to getting along rather than getting ahead, or they may question the system itself.

BROADER IMPLICATIONS: CLASS, CAPITALISM AND THE THIRD WORLD

It is difficult to generalize from a single case. In many respects, however, the findings from San Cosme are not unique. Many recent studies of industrialization, modernization, and development have concluded with the discouraging and superficially contradictory findings that some have benefitted and many have not. Chambers, for example, notes:

> nearly every Mesoamerican community study (and there are more than eighty of them, about half of which were published during the last ten years) has been directed in some respect to the problems of modernization in the hinterlands. But the hinterlands are still there, *disrupted as often as improved* by radical social changes which now seem to have widened rather than narrowed the gap between the powerful and the powerless. (1977:97, stress added)

The findings from San Cosme are another confirmation of the ill consequences and widening gap that go along with the improvements from capitalist industrialization. However, as Miliband suggests with regards to "bourgeois freedoms," it is a dangerous confusion, because of the inadequacy of the gains, to believe that they are of no consequence (Miliband 1969:267).

As Chambers notes, we will remain in a muddle with regards to both the meaning of contradictory findings and what to do about them until we relate the study of isolated cases to a more general description of social change (1977:97). This study has attempted to relate the case of San Cosme to a more general discussion of social change by using a class analysis. San Cosmeros must be seen as part of a larger capitalist system. At the international level, relations of dependence between Mexico and the advanced capitalist countries, especially the United States, have encouraged not only capitalism and a capitalist class structure but a dependent capitalism which is characterized by more poverty and a greater concentration of wealth. The possibilities for upward mobility in such a system are even more limited than in advanced capitalist countries.

Mainstream theorists often argue that "The description of component groups of a society in terms of 'classes'. . . is another relic of an earlier era [along with capitalism and socialism] that has ceased to serve a useful purpose" (Black 1966:52). They suggest instead that: "the best procedure seems to be to discard the older terminology and to use the more refined conceptions of occupational categories, social strata, and interest groups which have been developed in recent years by behavioral scientists" (Black 1966:52-53).

The hopes of San Cosmeros for occupational mobility for their children suggest that many San Cosmeros have adopted the "more refined conceptions of occupational categories." But they are also aware of the less refined concept of class and some of its consequences. There is also reason to believe that such an awareness is likely to be developing elsewhere in the Third World. Several years ago Sidney Mintz suggested that the countryside studied by anthropologists and others no longer consisted of a homogeneous peasant population. Many, he argued, had become a rural proletariat (1979:194). He noted also that this change was related to a movement from one stage of capitalism to another (1979:188).

It is becoming increasingly apparent that still another new stage of world capitalism is emerging. Large scale industry and monopoly capitalism are dominant not only in the core but, via the transnationals, are coming to dominate the periphery as well. As Helleiner suggests, "Manufacturing for export is the 'new frontier' for international business in the less-developed world" (1973:31). With the development of manufacture for export and the reloca- tion of industries from the core to the periphery, the *industrial* proletariat is growing. Along with this expansion of industrial capitalism the work force in the Third World is also becoming more stratified within as well as among nations. Even those not directly involved in the transnationals, such as the textile workers of San Cosme, are part of this stratified work force. Their position de- teriorates, not only as described earlier, because their jobs become simplified through the use of new imported technology, but also because of the differences in working conditions between monopoly capitalism and the competitive capitalism which continues to characterize some industry, such as the predominantly traditional Mexican textile industry.

The redivision of the labor force in the Third World is another step in the process by which the Third World is growing increas- ingly similar to the developed capitalist world. In 1980 San Cosme not only had domesticated women, child-centered families and proletarian men. While there, I watched the New York Yankees and "Wonder Woman" on television and listened to a woman born in San Cosme discussing the advantages of jogging shoes. The dependent or extroverted nature of capitalist industrialization in Mexico means, however, that a large part of the domestically produced surplus is transferred to repay foreign debts, to pay for foreign technology and parts, and to provide a profit to foreign investors. Any stratified society differentially distributes the society's products. In advanced capitalist societies, however, where much of the domestic surplus is not being transferred to another center, some benefits can be more widely distributed; there is still poverty and unemployment, and many of the available jobs are low paying and insecure. In a dependent capitalist nation, such as Mexico, where a "double tribute" is extracted from the working class to support foreign as well as local capitalists (Harding and Spalding 1976:8), there is more poverty, more unemployment, and more of the available jobs are low paying and insecure.

In their diverse ways, the women, men and children of San Cosme are all trying to avoid poverty, unemployment, and the least desirable jobs. At one level the new differentiation of the proletariat into homemakers, children, professionals and various other occupational categories divides the work force and prevents solidarity. At another level, however, it introduces the common hope that one's children will rise in the occupational hierarchy. San Cosmeros have not been passive victims of the expansion of industrial capitalism. They are subject to the redivision of the labor force, but they have very actively sought to improve the position at least of their children. There are hints that proletarians elsewhere in the Third World are similarly struggling for occupational mobility. If, however, success in the system is as limited as analysis of the new international division of labor suggests, workers as well as behavioral scientists may find the more "refined conceptions of occupational categories" less useful and turn instead to the less refined concept of class.

NOTES

1. See Sennett and Cobb (1972), Cardoso and Reyna (1968), Vellinga (1979), Boggs (1963) [cited by Sweezy (1972:165)], and Scrimshaw (1975).

2. There is a tendency for younger siblings to be more educated than their older siblings. Because the stress on education and the availability of secondary school are recent, however, it is difficult to determine whether this greater education of younger siblings is a consequence of the recency of the phenomenon or the necessity of having at least some children contributing wages to the family.

Bibliography

Abrams, Philip
>   1972   The Sense of the Past and the Origins of Sociology, *Past
>   and Present*. 55:18–32

Ariès, Philippe
>   1962   *Centuries of Childhood*. New York: Vintage.

Asamblea Popular de Desarrollo Estatal
>   1970   *Tlaxcala*. Tlaxcala: EIPES, CEPES.

Baird, Peter and Ed McCaughan
>   1977   Capital Shapes a New Workforce, *NACLA Report on the
>   Americas*. 11:20–24.

>   1979   *Beyond the Border*. New York: North American Congress
>   in Latin America.

Banco de Comercio
>   1970   *La Economía del Estado de Tlaxcala*. Mexico City: Banco
>   de Comercio.

Barkin, David
>   1971   La Educación: Una Barrera al Desarrollo Económico?
>   *El Trimestre Economico*. 38:951–983.

>   1975   Mexico's Albatross: The United States Economy, *Latin
>   American Perspectives*. 2:64–80.

Bartra, Roger
>   1974   *Estructura Agraria y Clases Sociales en México*. Mexico
>   City: Serie Popular Era (Instituto de Investigaciones
>   Sociales/UNAM).

>   1975   Peasants and Political Power in Mexico: A Theoretical
>   Model, *Latin American Perspectives*. 2:125–145.

Bastian, Walter
>   1979   Investing in Mexico, *Overseas Business Reports*. (May,
>   1979). Washington: U.S. Dept. of Commerce, Industry &
>   Trade Administration.

Beechey, Veronica
    1978   Women and Production: A Critical Analysis of Some
            Sociological Theories of Women's Work. In *Feminism and
            Materialism*, A. Kuhn & A. Wolpe (eds.), pp. 155–197.
            London: Routledge & Keegan Paul.
Belmonte, Thomas
    1979   *The Broken Fountain*. New York: Columbia University
            Press.
Berkner, Lutz
    1975   The Use and Misuse of Census Data for the Historical
            Analysis of Family Structure, *Journal of Interdisciplinary
            History*. 4:721–728.
Black, C. E.
    1966   *The Dynamics of Modernization*. New York: Harper &
            Row.
Boserup, Esther
    1970   *Women's Role in Economic Development*. London: George
            Allen & Unwin.
Brandenburg, Frank
    1964   *The Making of Modern Mexico*. Englewood Cliffs,
            N.J.: Prentice Hall.
Braverman, Harry
    1974   *Labor and Monopoly Capital*. New York: Monthly
            Review Press.
Cancian, Frank
    1965   *Economics and Prestige in a Mayan Community*. Stanford:
            Stanford University Press.
Cardoso, Fernando and Jose Reyna
    1968   Industrialization, Occupational Structure and Social
            Stratification in Latin America. In *Constructive Changes
            in Latin America*, C. Blasier (ed.), pp. 21–25. Pittsburgh:
            University of Pittsburgh Press.
Casanova, P. Gonzalez
    1970   *Democracy in Mexico*. New York: Oxford University
            Press.
Chambers, Erve
    1977   Modern Mesoamerica: The Politics of Identity, *American
            Anthropologist*. 79:92–97.
Chambers, Erve and P. Young
    1979   Mesoamerican Community Studies: The Past Decade.
            In *Annual Review of Anthropology*, B. Siegel, A. Beals,
            & S. Tylor (eds.), pp. 45–69. Palo Alto, Calif.: Annual
            Reviews, Inc.

Chayanov, A.V.
>   1966   *The Theory of Peasant Economy*. Homewood, Ill.:
>   Irwin.

Cline, Howard F.
>   1963   *Mexico*. New York: Oxford University Press.

Cockcroft, James
>   1974   Mexico. In *Latin America: The Struggle with Dependency
>   and Beyond*, R. Chilcote & J. Edelstein (eds.), pp. 222–
>   303. New York: John Wiley & Sons.

Cohen, Yehudi
>   1968   Culture as Adaptation. In *Man in Adaptation: The
>   Cultural Present*, Y. Cohen (ed.), pp. 40–60. Chicago:
>   Aldine.
>   1977   The Anthropological Enterprise, *American Anthro-
>   pologist*. 79:388–396.

Cornelius, Wayne
>   1977   Leaders, Followers and Official Patrons in Urban Mexico.
>   In *Friends, Followers, and Factions*, S. Schmidt, J. Scott,
>   C. Lande and L. Guasti (eds.), pp. 337–353. Berkeley:
>   University of California.

Deere, Carmen Diana
>   1979   Rural Women's Subsistence Production in the Capitalist
>   Periphery. In *Peasants and Proletarians*, R. Cohen, P. Gut-
>   kind, and P. Brazier (eds), pp. 133–148. New York:
>   Monthly Review Press.

de Janvry, Alain and Lynn Ground
>   1978   Types and Consequences of Land Reform in Latin Amer-
>   ica, *Latin American Perspectives*. 5:90–112.

DeWalt, Billie R.
>   1979   *Modernization in a Mexican Ejido*. London: Cambridge
>   University Press.

Dietz, James L.
>   1979   Imperialism and Underdevelopment: A Theoretical
>   Perspective and a Case Study of Puerto Rico, *The Review
>   of Racial Political Economics*. 2:16–32.

Dirección General de Estadistíca
>   1940   *VII Censo General de Población*. Mexico City: Secre-
>   taría de Industria y Comercio.
>   1950   *VII Censo General de Población*. Mexico City: Secretaría
>   de Industria y Comercio.
>   1960   *VIII Censo General de Población*: Mexico City: Secretaría
>   de Industria y Comercio.

1970   *IX Censo General de Población.* Mexico City: Secretaría de Industria y Comercio.

Dirección General de Planeacion Educativa
1975   *Tlaxcala: Sistema Educativo.* Mexico City: Secretaría de Educación.

Eckstein, Susan
1977   *The Poverty of Revolution.* Princeton: Princeton University Press.

Economic Commission for Latin America
1978   *Economic Survey of Latin America: 1977.* Santiago, Chile: United Nations.

Edelman, Marc
1980   Agricultural Modernization in Smallholding Areas of Mexico: A Case Study in the Sierra Norte de Puebla, *Latin American Perspectives.* 7:29–49.

Edwards, Richard, David Gordon and Michael Reich (eds.)
1971   *The Capitalist System.* Englewood Cliffs, N.J.: Prentice Hall.

Ehrenreich, Barbara and Annette Fuentas
1981   Special Report: Life on the Global Assembly Line, *Ms.* 9:52–59.

Elder, Glen H., Jr.
1978   Approaches to Social Change and the Family. In *Turning Points,* John Demos and S. Spence Boocock (eds.), pp. S1–S38. Chicago: University of Chicago Press. (*American Journal of Sociology,* volume 84, supplement, 1978).

Fagen, Richard and William Tuohy
1972   *Politics and Privilege in a Mexican City.* Stanford: Stanford University.

Fernandez-Kelly, Patricia
1980   The 'Maquila' Women, *NACLA Report on the Americas.* 14:14–19.

n.d.   Francisca Lucero: A Profile of Female Factory Work in Ciudad Juarez. Unpublished manuscript.

Foster-Carter, Aiden
1978   The Modes of Production Controversy, *New Left Review.* 107:47–78.

Frank, Andre Gunder
1969a   *Capitalism and Underdevelopment in Latin America.* New York: Monthly Review Press.

1969b   *Latin America: Underdevelopment and Revolution.* New York: Monthly Review Press.

Galbraith, John Kenneth
    1973   *Economics and the Public Purpose*. Boston: Houghton Mifflin Co.

Gintis, Herbert
    1971   Education, Technology, and the Characteristics of Worker Productivity, *American Economic Review*. 61:266–279.

Gladwin, Christiana
    1979   Production Functions and Decision Models: Complementary Models, *American Ethnologist*. 6:653–674.

Gollás, Manuel and Adalberto García Rocha
    1976   El Desarrollo Económico Reciente de México. In *Contemporary Mexico*, J. Wilkie, M. Meyer, and E. Monzon de Wilkie (eds.), pp. 405–440. Berkeley: University of California.

Grindle, Merilee S.
    1977   Patrons and Clients in the Bureaucracy, *Latin American Research Review*. 12:37–66.

Hall, Anthony.
    1977   Patron-Client Relations: Concepts and Terms. In *Friends, Followers, and Factions*, S. Schmidt, J. Scott, C. Lande, and L. Guasti (eds.), pp. 510–512. Berkeley: University of California.

Hansen, Roger
    1971   *The Politics of Mexican Development*. Baltimore: Johns Hopkins University Press.

Harding, Timothy
    1976   *Organized Labor in Latin America*. New York: Harper & Row.

Harding, Timothy and Hobart Spalding
    1976   The Struggle Sharpens: Workers, Imperialism and the State in Latin America, Common Themes and New Directions, *Latin American Perspectives*. 3:3–14.

Harris, Marvin
    1979   *Cultural Materialism*. New York: Random House.

Helleiner, G. K.
    1973   Manufactured Exports from Less-Developed Countries and Multinational Firms, *The Economic Journal*. 83:21–47.

Hewitt de Alcantara, Cynthia
    1974   *La Modernización de la Agricultura Mexicana, 1940–1970*. Mexico City: Siglo Veintiuno.

Hofstadter, Dan
    1974   *Mexico 1946–1973*. New York: Facts on File.

Holt, Elizabeth and Lilia Padilla
1975   *Analfabetismo y Escorlaridad en el Estado de Tlaxcala.*
Mexico City: UNAM Facultad de Filsofiá y Letras,
Centro de las Investigaciónes Geográficas.

Horowitz, Irving Louis
1972   *Three Worlds of Development.* New York: Oxford University Press.

Hughes, Jon
1970   *Industrialization and Economic History.* New York:
McGraw-Hill.

Johnson, Allan
1972   *Modernization and Social Change.* Unpublished Ph.D.
dissertation, University of Michigan.

Johnson, Allen W.
1978   *Quantification in Cultural Anthropology.* Stanford:
Stanford University Press.

Johnson, Dale
1972   On Oppressed Classes. In *Dependence and Underdevelopment: Latin America's Political Economy,* J. Cockcroft, A.G. Frank, and D. Johnson (eds.), pp. 269–301.
New York: Anchor Books.

Johnson, Kenneth
1971   *Mexican Democracy.* Boston: Allyn & Bacon.

Juárez, Antonio
1979   *Las Corporaciones Transnacionales y los Trabajadores
Mexicanos.* Mexico City: Siglo Veintiuno.

Kahl, Joseph
1968   *The Measurement of Modernism: A Study of Values in
Brazil and Mexico.* Austin: University of Texas Press.

Katz, Michael and Ian Davey
1978   Youth and Early Industrialization in a Canadian City.
In *Turning Points,* J. Demos and S. Spence Boocock (eds.),
pp. S81–S119. Chicago: University of Chicago (*American
Journal of Sociology,* supplement volume 84, 1978).

Kay, Geoffrey
1975   *Development and Underdevelopment: A Marxist Analysis.*
New York: St. Martin's Press.

Klass, Morton
1978   *From Field to Factory: Community Structure and Industrialization in West Bengal.* Philadelphia: Institute
for the Study of Human Issues.

Kumar, Krishan
1978   *Prophecy and Progress.* Middlesex, Eng.: Penguin Books.

Lange, Oskar
    1968   Marxian Economics and Modern Economic Theory. In
            Marx and Modern Economics, D. Horowitz (ed.), pp.
            68–87. New York: Monthly Review Press.
Laslett, Peter and R. Wall, eds.
    1972   *Household and the Family in Past Time*. London: Cam-
            bridge University Press.
Leacock, Eleanor
    1981   *Myths of Male Dominance*. New York: Monthly Review
            Press.
Leal, Juan Felipe
    1975   The Political Economy of the Mexican State, *Latin Amer-
            ican Perspectives*. 2:48–63.
Lewis, Oscar
    1952   Urbanization without Breakdown: A Case Study, *The
            Scientific Monthly*. 75:31–41.
    1963   *Life in a Mexican Village: Tepoztlan Restudied*. Urbana:
            University of Illinois Press.
    1968   The Culture of Poverty. In *Poverty in America*, L. Ferman,
            J. Kornbluh, and A. Haber (eds.), pp. 405–415. Ann
            Arbor: University of Michigan Press.
Lomnitz, Larissa
    1977   *Networks and Marginality*. New York: Academic Press.
Marx, Karl
    1967   *Capital*, Volume I. New York: International Publishers.
Mesa-Lago, Carmelo
    1976   Social Security Stratification and Inequality in Mexico.
            In *Contemporary Mexico*, J. Wilkie, M. Meyer, and E.
            Monzon de Wilkie (eds.), pp. 228–255. Berkeley: Uni-
            versity of California.
Miliband, Ralph
    1969   *The State in Capitalist Society*. New York: Basic Books.
Miller, Frank
    1973   *Old Villages and a New Town: Industrialization in
            Mexico*. Menlo Park, California: Cummings Publishing.
Minge-Kalman, Wanda
    1978   The Industrial Revolution and the European Family: The
            Institutionalization of "Childhood" as a Market Factor
            for Family Labor, *Comparative Studies in Society and
            History*, 20:454–468.
Mintz, Sidney
    1979   The Rural Proletariat and the Problem of the Rural Pro-
            letarian Consciousness. In *Peasants and Proletarians*,

R. Cohen, P. Gutkind, and P. Brazer (eds.), pp. 173–198. New York: Monthly Review Press.

Moore, Wilbert
1963   *Social Change*. Englewood Cliffs, N.J.: Prentice-Hall.

Muñoz, Humberto Garcia
1975   *Occupational and Earnings Inequalities in Mexico City: A Sectoral Analysis of the Labor Force*. Unpublished Ph.D. dissertation. University of Texas at Austin.

Myrdal, Gunnar
1971   Regional Economic Inequalities. In *Economic Development and Social Change*, G. Dalton (ed.), pp. 375–386. Garden City, N.Y.: The Natural History Press.

Nash, June
1979   *We Eat the Mines and the Mines Eat Us*. New York: Columbia University Press.

Nash, Manning
1967   *Machine Age Maya*. Chicago: University of Chicago Press.

Nava, Luis
1978   *Tlaxcala Contemporánea 1822–1977*. Mexico City: Editorial Progreso.

Needler, Martin
1971   *Politics and Society in Mexico*. Albuquerque: University of New Mexico.

Nelson, Cynthia
1971   *The Waiting Village*. Boston: Little, Brown and Company.

Niblo, Stephen R.
1975   Progress and the Standard of Living in Mexico, *Latin American Perspectives*. 2:109–124.

Nutini, Hugo
1968   *San Bernardino Contla*. Pittsburgh: University of Pittsburgh Press.

Nutini, Hugo and Timothy Murphy
1970   Labor Migration and Family Structure in the Tlaxcala-Pueblan Area, Mexico. In *The Social Anthropology of Latin America*, W. Goldschmidt and H. Hoijer (eds.), pp. 80–103. Los Angeles: University of California.

Owen, R. and B. Sutcliffe, eds.
1972   *Studies in Theories of Imperialism*. London: Longman.

Paré, Luisa
1975   *El Plan Puebla: Una Revolución Verde que Está Muy Verde*. Chapingo, Mexico: Ediciones de Sociología Rural.

Radice, Hugo (Ed.)
　　1975　*International Firms and Modern Imperialism.* Harmonds-
　　　　　worth, England: Penguin.

Redclift, Michael
　　1980　Agrarian Populism in Mexico—the 'Via Campesina,'
　　　　　Journal of Peasant Studies. 7:492–502.

Roberts, Robert E.
　　1973　Modernization and Infant Mortality in Mexico, *Econom-
　　　　　ic Development and Cultural Change.* 21:665–669.

Rogers, Everett
　　1975　The Anthropology of Modernization and the
　　　　　Modernization of Anthropology, *Reviews in Anthro-
　　　　　pology.* 2:345–358.

Rothstein, Frances
　　1975　Differential Integration: A Comparison of the Economic,
　　　　　Political, and Social Relations of Peasants and Factory
　　　　　Workers, *Ethnology.* 4:395–404.
　　1979　The Class Basis of Patron-Client Relations, *Latin American
　　　　　Perspectives.* 6:25–35.

Safa, Helen Icken
　　1976　Class Consciousness among Working-Class Women in
　　　　　Latin America: A Case Study in Puerto Rico. In *Sex and
　　　　　Class in Latin America,* June Nash and Helen Icken Safa
　　　　　(eds.), pp. 69–85. New York: Praeger Publishers.
　　1978　Women, Production and Reproduction in Industrial
　　　　　Capitalism: A Comparison of Brazilian and U.S. Factory
　　　　　Workers. Draft paper prepared for the Conference on the
　　　　　Continuing Subordination of Women and the Develop-
　　　　　ment Process (Sussex, England).
　　1979　Multinationals and the Employment of Women in De-
　　　　　veloping Areas: The Case of the Caribbean. Paper
　　　　　prepared for the Latin American Studies Association
　　　　　(Pittsburgh).

Sanders, Thomas
　　1974a　Mexico 1974: Demographis Patterns and Population
　　　　　Policy, *Fieldstaff Reports* 2(1):1–28. Hanover, N.H.:
　　　　　American Universities Field Staff.
　　1974b　CIMMYT: Agricultural Innovation in Mexico, *Field-
　　　　　staff Reports.* 2(6):1–17. Hanover, N.H.: American Uni-
　　　　　versities Field Staff.
　　1975　Mexico's Food Problem, *Fieldstaff Reports* 3(1):1–18.
　　　　　Hanover, N.H.: American Universities Field Staff.

Schildkrout, Enid
    1981   Young Traders of Northern Nigeria, *Natural History*.
            90:44–53.
Schwartz, Norman B.
    1978   Community Development and Cultural Change in Latin
            America. In *Annual Review of Anthropology*, B. Siegel,
            A. Beals, and S. Tylor (eds.), pp. 235–263. Palo Alto,
            California: Annual Reviews, Inc.
Scott, James C.
    1977   Patron-Client Politics and Political Change in Southeast
            Asia. In *Friends, Followers, and Factions*, S. Schmidt,
            J. Scott, C. Lande, and L. Guasti (eds.), pp. 123–146.
            Berkeley: University of California.
Scott, R.
    1959   *Mexican Government in Transition*. Urbana: University
            of Illinois.
Scrimshaw, Susan
    1975   A Study of Changing Values, Fertility, and Socio-economic
            Status. In *Population and Social Organization*, M. Nag
            (ed.). The Hague: Mouton.
Sen, Gita
    1980   The Sexual Division of Labor and the Working-Class
            Family: Towards a Conceptual Synthesis of Class Rela-
            tions and the Subordination of Women, *The Review of
            Political Economics*. 12:76–86.
Sennett, Richard and Jonathan Cobb
    1972   *The Hidden Injuries of Class*. New York: Vintage.
Shanin, Teodor
    1971   *The Awkward Class*. London: Clarendon Press.
Shorter, Edward
    1975   *The Making of the Modern Family*. New York: Basic
            Books.
Smelser, Neil
    1971   Mechanisms of Change and Adjustment to Change. In
            Economic Development and Social Change, G. Dalton
            (eds.), pp. 352–374. Garden City, N.Y.: The Natural
            History Press.
Sokoloff, Natalie
    1980   *Between Money and Love*. New York: Praeger.
Sorokin, P., C. Zimmerman and C. J. Galpin
    1930   *A Systematic Source Book in Rural Sociology*. Minne-
            apolis: University of Minnesota Press.

Stevens, Evelyn P.
    1974   *Protest and Response in Mexico*. Cambridge, Mass.:
            MIT Press.

Stuart, William
    1972   The Explanation of Patron-Client Systems. In *Structure
            and Process in Latin America*, A Strickon and S. Green-
            field (eds.), pp. 19–42. Albuquerque: University of New
            Mexico.

Sweezy, Paul M.
    1972   Modern Capitalism and Other Essays. New York:
            Monthly Review Press.

Taylor, Philip B.
    1960   The Mexican Election of 1958: Affirmation of Authori-
            tarianism? *Western Political Quarterly*. 13:722–744.

Thompson, E. P.
    1966   *The Making of the English Working Class*. New York:
            Random House.

Tilly, Louise and Joan Scott
    1978   *Women, Work, and Family*. New York: Holt, Rinehart
            and Winston.

Tipps, Dean C.
    1973   Modernization Theory and the Study of National Societies:
            A Critical Perspective, *Comparative Studies in Society
            and History*. 15:199–226.

Valentine, Charles
    1972   Black Studies and Anthropology: Scholarly and Political
            Interests, Addison-Wesley Module, No. 15. Reading,
            Mass.: Addison-Wesley Publishing Company.

van Ginneken, Wouter
    1979   Socio-Economic Groups and Income Distribution in
            Mexico, *International Labour Review*. 118:331–342.

Vellinga, Menno
    1979   *Industrialización Burgesía y Clase Obrera en México*.
            Mexico City: Siglo Veintiuno.

Wells, Robert
    1978   Family History and Demographic Transition. In *The
            American Family in Social-Historical Perspective*. M.
            Gordon (ed.), pp. 516–532. New York: St. Martin's.

Wolf, Eric
    1955   Types of Latin American Peasantry. *American Anthro-
            pologist*. 57:452–471.

Yanagisako, Sylvia Junko
    1979   Family and Household: The Analysis of Domestic Groups.
            In *Annual Review of Anthropology*, B. Siegel, A. Beals,
            and S. Tylor (eds.), pp. 161–205. Palo Alto, Calif.:
            Annual Reviews Inc.

Index

About the Author

FRANCES ABRAHAMER ROTHSTEIN is Associate Professor of Sociology and Anthropology at Towson State University. She has authored articles on family life and industrialization which have appeared in *Social Science and Medicine, Ethnology,* and *Latin American Perspectives*. Professor Rothstein also served as coeditor, with Professor Madeline Barbara Leons, for *New Directions in Political Economy: An Approach from Anthropology* (Greenwood Press, 1979).